A TASTE OF THE COUNTRY

Editor: Jean Van Dyke
Food Editor: Grace Howaniec
Art Director: Jim Sibilski
Art Associate: Judy Larson
Production: Sally Manich, Ellen Baltes
Food Photography: Mike Huibregtse

International Standard Book Number: 0-89821-091-7
Library of Congress Catalog Card Number: 90-62428
© 1990, Reiman Associates Inc.
5400 S. 60th St., Greendale, WI 53129
All rights reserved.
Printed in U.S.A.

Dishes on cover are pictured on Pages 24 and 25.

Ahh, comfort foods...those old-fashioned favorites Mom served up with ample portions of love. These recipes take you back to kitchens filled with feel-good foods that made bad days better and good days great.

Remember homemade doughnuts? The rich, yeasty aroma of those golden-brown beauties, fried in a cast-iron kettle, made for a wonderful welcome home from school.

Recall Mom's savory meat loaf? It was always filling and substantial, topped with a sweet-sour catsup sauce and served with potatoes, gravy and green beans. What a treat!

And how about made-from-scratch macaroni and cheese...soothing chicken soup...raisin-and-spice-studded noodle pudding...and hearty stick-to-your-ribs muffins! For dessert,

there was light, custardy bread pudding with lemon sauce.

Remember? If you don't, just try these flavorful comfort food favorites. They'll take you home in memory.

In the chips! Mmmm…nothing comforts and cheers like a really good chocolate chip cookie. And there's a variation for every taste! Choose from a classic drop cookie, a dark and decadent fudgy variety, a brown-sugar-meringue-topped bar cookie or a rich, exotic cookie chewy with coconut and macadamia nuts.

COMFORTING COOKIES: Top to bottom—**Classic Chocolate Chip Cookies,** Lois Miller, Fredericksburg, Pennsylvania (Pg. 12); **Island Treasure Cookies,** Dorothy Schafer, Nazareth, Pennsylvania (Pg. 12); **Chewy Chocolate Chip Bars,** Gloria Secor, Kenosha, Wisconsin (Pg. 12); and **Double Chocolate Chip Cookies,** Glenna Tooman, Boise, Idaho (Pg. 13).

MEALS IN MINUTES

SOUTH-OF-THE-BORDER taste and ready-in-no-time convenience combine to make this menu a busy cook's dream!

Begin by mixing up the instant pudding/pie filling and spooning it into the prepared shell. Pop the pie into the freezer for fast setting.

Then, quickly brown the ground beef, chop the onion and combine the soup ingredients. As the soup simmers, prepare the simple salad of iceberg lettuce with tomato and cucumber slices. Use a purchased sour cream dressing.

Ladle the soup into bowls, top it with grated cheese and serve taco or corn chips in place of crackers. It's a hearty, satisfying main course soup—like chili, but without the wait.

TACO SOUP

1-1/2 pounds ground beef
1/2 cup chopped onion
1 can (28 ounces) whole tomatoes with juice
1 can (14 ounces) kidney beans with juice
1 can (17 ounces) corn with juice
1 can (8 ounces) tomato sauce
1 package taco seasoning
1 to 2 cups water
Salt and pepper to taste
1 cup grated cheddar cheese

Brown beef in large heavy kettle; drain and add onions. Cook until onions are tender. Add remaining ingredients except cheese; simmer for 15 minutes. Ladle into bowls; top with the grated cheese. **Yield:** 6-8 servings.

GARDEN SALAD

1 head iceberg lettuce, rinsed and chilled
1 large cucumber, washed
2 tomatoes, cut in wedges
Commercial sour cream dressing

Slice lettuce into 1/2-in.-thick chunks. Score unpeeled cucumber with fork; cut into thin slices. Place the tomato wedges and cucumber slices on the lettuce; top with dressing. **Yield:** 6 servings.

CHOCOLATE CREAM PIE

1 pastry crust *or* crumb crust (9 inches), baked
FILLING:
1 package (4-1/8 ounces) instant chocolate fudge pudding
2 cups milk
1 cup whipping cream, *divided*
1 chocolate bar, chopped
Mint leaves

Combine the pudding mix and milk according to package directions. Let stand for 5 minutes. Meanwhile, whip cream. Add half of whipped cream to pudding, reserving remaining cream for garnish. Place pie in freezer for 5 minutes; refrigerate until time to eat. Garnish top of pie with remaining whipped cream and chopped chocolate and mint leaves. **Yield:** 6 servings.

JERRY'S SECRET PORK CHOP MARINADE

Jerry Wiebel, Fort Atkinson, Wisconsin

3/4 cups soy sauce (may use lite soy sauce, if preferred)
1/4 cup fresh lemon juice
1 tablespoon chili sauce
1 tablespoon brown sugar
1 clove garlic, *minced*

6 pork loin chops, cut 1-1/4 inches thick

Combine marinade ingredients. Place pork chops in glass baking dish or heavy plastic zip-lock bag; add marinade. Cover dish with plastic wrap or close bag. Marinate chops overnight in refrigerator, turning occasionally. Grill or broil chops over medium heat for 8-10 minutes per side. Turn and brush occasionally with reserved marinade. Garnish with fresh lemon twists and parsley, if desired. **Yield:** 6 servings.

It's not just for the holidays anymore! Turkey has taken center stage in plenty of country kitchens, as cooks put scrumptious and surprisingly new twists on turkey these days —serving it up as soups, salads and suppertime stars. Try some of these fresh approaches...enjoy these turkey treats!

TASTY TURKEY: Clockwise from lower left—**Hot Turkey Taco Salad,** Jean Bergin, Mishicot, Wisconsin (Pg. 13); **Barbecued Turkey,** Holly Petersen, Hunter, North Dakota (Pg. 13); **Grilled Turkey Steaks,** Barbara Wellnitz, Ashby, Minnesota (Pg. 14); **Grilled Turkey Tenderloin,** Helen Miller, Teutopolis, Illinois (Pg. 14); **Stir-Fry Turkey With Walnuts,** Terri Holmgren, Swanville, Minnesota (Pg. 14); **Day-After Turkey Pie,** Kay Smith, Gooding, Idaho (Pg. 15); **Turkey Scallopini,** JoAnne Hill, Lisbon, Maryland (Pg. 14); **Turkey Ham Quiche/Hash Brown Crust,** Dana Tegtmeier, Bern, Kansas (Pg. 13).

Turkey has taken on a whole new role—moving from its place as centerpiece at holiday feasts to a tasty, easy-to-prepare addition to everyday menus.

These four flavorful turkey dishes will be a hit with your family… whether you serve creamy Williamsburg Inn Turkey Soup, spicy Turkey Enchiladas, refreshingly different Tangy Turkey Salad or Turkey Piccata—a new twist on a dinnertime classic. Enjoy the taste of turkey —any day of the year.

TURKEY TREATS: Bottom to top —**Turkey Piccata,** Perlene Hoekema, Lynden, Washington; **Turkey Enchiladas,** Jo Groth, Plainfield, Iowa; **Tangy Turkey Salad,** Merridy Kienitz, Blue Earth, Minnesota; **Williamsburg Inn Turkey Soup,** Muriel Lerdal, Humboldt, Iowa. (All recipes can be found on Page 15.)

MY FAVORITE BRAN MUFFINS
Rosemary Smith, Fort Bragg, California

(PICTURED ON PAGE 4)

1-1/4 cups unprocessed bran*
1 cup toasted wheat germ
1 cup brown sugar
2-1/2 cups whole wheat flour
2-1/2 teaspoons baking soda
1/2 teaspoon salt
1 tablespoon grated orange peel
2 eggs, slightly beaten
1/2 cup honey
1/4 cup molasses
1/2 cup vegetable oil
2 cups buttermilk
1 cup boiling water

In large bowl, combine bran, wheat germ, sugar, flour, baking soda, salt and orange peel; set aside. Combine eggs, honey, molasses, oil, buttermilk and boiling water; mix well with dry ingredients. Spoon batter into greased muffin tins, filling 2/3 full. Bake at 350° for 20-25 minutes. Batter may be made ahead and stored in refrigerator for up to 1 month to be used as needed. *You may substitute Mueslix cereal for part of the bran. **Yield:** 2 dozen muffins.

SWEDISH RYE BREAD
Marilyn Young, Marquette, Kansas

(PICTURED ON PAGE 4)

2 packages active dry yeast
1/2 cup warm water (110-115°)
1 teaspoon sugar
1-1/2 cups rye flour
1/2 cup sugar
3 teaspoons salt
3 cups hot water
1/2 cup melted vegetable shortening
1/2 cup molasses
9-1/4 cups white flour

Dissolve yeast in warm water; stir in 1 teaspoon sugar. Set aside. In large mixing bowl, mix rye flour with 1/2 cup sugar and salt. Add hot water gradually, mixing to a smooth paste. Gradually add melted shortening and molasses; beat well. Add yeast mixture and white flour. When dough becomes too stiff to work with spoon, knead in remaining flour until dough is smooth and elastic. Place in warm area until doubled in bulk. Divide into three loaves and place in greased 9-in. x 5-in. x 3-in. pans. Let rise until double. Bake at

325° for 40 minutes. Remove from pans; rub tops and sides of bread with melted shortening. **Yield:** 3 loaves.

BUTTERMILK DOUGHNUTS
Judy Jungwirth, Athol, South Dakota

(PICTURED ON PAGE 4)

1 package active dry yeast
1/4 cup warm water (110-115°)
3/4 cup scalded buttermilk
1/4 cup sugar
1 teaspoon salt
1/4 cup shortening
1/2 cup fresh mashed potato
1 egg, beaten
1 teaspoon nutmeg
3-1/2 to 4 cups all-purpose flour

Dissolve yeast in water; set aside. Combine remaining ingredients; stir in yeast. Knead 5 minutes until smooth. Let rise until double. Roll out on floured board to 1/2-in. thickness. Cut doughnuts with cutter. Let rise 30-35 minutes. Fry in hot oil until brown on both sides. Drain on paper towels. Dust with sugar, if desired. **Yield:** About 24 doughnuts.

NOODLE KUGEL
Sally Stapleton, Milwaukee, Wisconsin

(PICTURED ON PAGE 5)

12 ounces flat egg noodles
3 eggs
1/4 cup sugar
2/3 cup hoop or farmer's cheese, crumbled
1/2 teaspoon salt
1/2 teaspoon cinnamon
1/4 teaspoon nutmeg
1/2 cup dairy sour cream
1/2 cup golden raisins
1/4 cup butter, *divided*

Preheat oven to 350°. Cook noodles in boiling salted water for 8 to 10 minutes or until tender but not soft. Drain; set aside. Beat together eggs, sugar, cheese, salt, cinnamon, nutmeg, sour cream and raisins; set aside. Cut *one-half* of butter into small bits. Stir together noodles, egg/cheese mixture and cut-up butter. Put 1 teaspoon butter in 3-qt. casserole; heat in oven until butter melts. Tilt casserole to coat sides with butter. Spoon in kugel mixture. Sprinkle with additional cinnamon; dot with the remaining butter. Bake at 350° for 25-30 minutes or until golden brown. **Yield:** 6-8 servings.

HOMEMADE CHICKEN NOODLE SOUP
Rita Eipperle, Omaha, Nebraska

(PICTURED ON PAGE 5)

BROTH:
1 fryer chicken (3 to 4 pounds)
1 large onion, chopped into bite-sized pieces
1 cup celery, chopped into bite-sized pieces
1 cup carrots, chopped into bite-sized pieces
2 tablespoons chicken bouillon granules
1/2 teaspoon fresh ground pepper
2 quarts water (approximately)
2 tablespoons freshly snipped parsley
1/2 teaspoon dried lemon thyme, *optional*
1 cup dry noodles, precooked according to package directions
Salt, pepper to taste

Wash and drain chicken; place in large soup kettle with onion, celery, carrots, bouillon and pepper. Add enough cold water to just cover chicken. Simmer 1 hour or until chicken is tender. Remove chicken from broth; discard skin, fat, bones and cartilage. Reserve all meat; cut or shred as you prefer. Return meat to broth; add parsley, lemon thyme, precooked noodles of choice and salt, pepper to taste. Reheat broth to desired temperature. **Yield:** 3 quarts soup.

MACARONI AND CHEESE
Betty Mantz, Philipsburg, Pennsylvania

(PICTURED ON PAGE 5)

1 cup dry macaroni
1 cup cottage cheese
1 cup dairy sour cream
1 cup Velveeta cheese, cut up
1 cup sharp cheddar cheese, grated
2 eggs, beaten

Cook macaroni according to package directions; drain. Combine cottage cheese, sour cream, Velveeta, cheddar cheese and eggs in buttered 2-1/2-qt. casserole. Add cooked macaroni; fold in thoroughly. Bake at 350° for 45 minutes. **Yield:** 6-8 servings.

SWEET-AND-SOUR MEAT LOAF
Debbie Haneke, Stafford, Kansas

(PICTURED ON PAGE 5)

1-1/2 pounds ground beef
1 cup dry bread crumbs
1 teaspoon salt
1/4 teaspoon pepper
2 eggs
1 teaspoon instant minced onion
1 can (15 ounces) tomato sauce, *divided*

TOPPING:
Reserved tomato sauce
2 tablespoons brown sugar
2 tablespoons vinegar
1/2 cup sugar
2 teaspoons prepared mustard

Mix together beef, bread crumbs, salt, pepper and eggs. Add onions and one-half of tomato sauce. Form into loaf in 9-in. x 5-in. x 3-in. pan. Bake at 350° for 50 minutes. In saucepan, combine topping ingredients; bring to boil. Pour over meat loaf; bake 10 minutes more. **Yield:** 6 servings.

BREAD PUDDING
Bernice Harder, Moline, Illinois

(PICTURED ON PAGE 5)

2 cups day-old bread cubes, crusts removed, cut 1/4- to 1/2-inch
2 cups milk
1/4 cup sugar
3 tablespoons butter
2 eggs
Dash salt
1/2 teaspoon vanilla

LEMON SAUCE:
3/4 to 1 cup sugar
2 tablespoons cornstarch
1/8 teaspoon salt
2 cups water
1 tablespoon grated lemon peel
1/4 cup butter
2 tablespoons fresh lemon juice

Place bread cubes in buttered 1-1/2-qt. baking dish (or individual ramekins, as shown); set aside. In small saucepan, mix and heat milk, sugar and butter just enough to dissolve sugar and melt butter. Beat eggs slightly, adding salt to mixture. Stir eggs into warm milk and add vanilla. Pour liquid mixture over bread cubes and set baking dishes in a pan of hot water. Bake at 350° for 1 hour or until a knife inserted in center comes out clean. While pudding bakes, prepare lemon sauce by combining sugar, cornstarch and salt in saucepan. Stir in water and lemon peel; boil for 1 minute. Remove from heat and stir in butter and lemon juice. Serve pudding hot with lemon sauce. **Yield:** 6 servings.

CLASSIC CHOCOLATE CHIP COOKIES
Lois Miller, Fredericksburg, Pennsylvania

(PICTURED ON PAGE 6)

2-1/4 cups flour
1 teaspoon baking soda
1 cup butter *or* margarine, softened
1/4 cup granulated sugar
3/4 cup brown sugar
1 teaspoon vanilla
1 package (3-1/2 ounces) vanilla flavor *instant* pudding
2 eggs
1 package (12 ounces) semisweet chocolate chips
1 cup chopped walnuts, optional

Combine flour and baking soda; set aside. Combine butter, sugars, vanilla and pudding mix in large mixer bowl; beat until smooth and creamy. Beat in eggs; gradually add flour mixture. Stir in chocolate chips and nuts (batter will be stiff). Drop by heaping teaspoonsful, about 2 inches apart, onto ungreased cookie sheets. Bake at 375° for 9 to 9-1/2 minutes or until browned. **Yield:** 4-1/2 dozen cookies, 2-1/2-inches in diameter.

CHEWY CHOCOLATE CHIP BARS
Gloria Secor, Kenosha, Wisconsin

(PICTURED ON PAGE 6)

1 cup butter, room temperature
1/2 cup granulated sugar
1 cup brown sugar, *divided*
1 tablespoon water
1 teaspoon vanilla
2 eggs, *separated*
2 cups flour
1/2 teaspoon salt
1/2 teaspoon baking soda
1 teaspoon baking powder
3/4 cup semisweet chocolate chips
3/4 cup *finely* chopped walnuts

Cream together butter, granulated sugar and *1/2 cup brown sugar* until light and fluffy. Add water, vanilla and egg *yolks* (reserve whites in separate bowl); beat for 2-3 minutes. Beat in flour, salt, baking soda and powder. Spread batter onto lightly greased 13-in. x 9-in. x 2-in. baking pan *or* jelly roll pan. Sprinkle on chocolate chips. Beat egg whites until they form soft peaks, then add reserved brown sugar, blending well. Carefully spread over chips. Sprinkle with chopped nuts. Bake at 350° for 35 minutes or until meringue is light brown. Cut with sharp knife while still hot. **Yield:** 3 dozen bars.

ISLAND TREASURE COOKIES
Dorothy Schafer, Nazareth, Pennsylvania

(PICTURED ON PAGE 6)

1-2/3 cups all-purpose flour
3/4 teaspoon baking powder
3/4 teaspoon salt
1/2 teaspoon baking soda
3/4 cup *plus* 2 tablespoons butter, softened
3/4 cup brown sugar
1/3 cup granulated sugar
3/4 teaspoon vanilla
1 egg
3/4 cup (2 ounces) toasted coconut
3/4 cup (3-1/2 ounces) chopped macadamia nuts
1 package (11-1/2 ounces) milk chocolate chips

Combine flour, baking powder, salt and baking soda; set aside. In medium mixing bowl, beat butter, sugars and vanilla until creamy. Add egg; mix well. Gradually add flour mixture. Stir in coconut, macadamia nuts and milk chocolate chips. Drop by heaping tablespoons, 3 inches apart, onto ungreased cookie sheets. Bake at 375° for 12 minutes or until lightly browned. Allow to stand for 2 minutes before removing from cookie sheets. **Yield:** 32 cookies, each 3-1/2 inches.

CUT OUT CRYSTALS: To keep sugar crystals from sticking to sides of your pan during cooking, butter the sides first, bring candy mixture to a boil and cover the pan for 2-3 minutes until enough steam forms to force sugar crystals from sides. Then uncover and cook as usual.

DOUBLE CHOCOLATE
CHIP COOKIES
Glenna Tooman, Boise, Idaho

(PICTURED ON PAGE 6)

8 squares (1 ounce each)
    semisweet chocolate
3 squares (1 ounce each)
    unsweetened chocolate
6 tablespoons butter *or* margarine
1/3 cup flour
1/4 teaspoon baking powder
1/4 teaspoon salt
3 eggs
1 cup sugar
2 teaspoons vanilla
1-1/2 cups semisweet chocolate chips
1 cup chopped pecans
1 cup chopped walnuts

Melt semisweet and unsweetened chocolates together with butter/margarine over low heat, stirring until smooth. Cool. Sift together flour, baking powder and salt; set aside. Beat eggs, sugar and vanilla until slightly thickened. Add the melted chocolate, mixing well. Add flour mixture, mixing well. Stir in chocolate chips, pecans and walnuts. (If batter is thin, allow to stand for 10 minutes.) Drop by heaping tablespoonfuls onto lightly greased cookie sheets, spacing cookies 3 inches apart. Bake at 350° for 8-10 minutes. Remove to rack to cool. *Do not overbake.* **Yield:** 3 dozen cookies.

TURKEY HAM QUICHE/
HASH BROWN CRUST
Dana Tegtmeier, Bern, Kansas

(PICTURED ON PAGE 8)

CRUST:
3 cups cubed frozen hash
    brown potatoes, *defrosted*
1/2 cup onion, chopped, *divided*
2 tablespoons green pepper,
    finely chopped
1/8 teaspoon white pepper
1 egg, beaten
FILLING:
1-1/2 cups *turkey ham*, diced
1 cup (4 ounces) Swiss cheese,
    grated
1 cup milk (can use skim or 2%)
4 eggs
2 teaspoons prepared mustard
1/4 teaspoon white pepper

In medium bowl, combine potatoes, *1/4 cup* onion, green pepper and white pepper. Fold in beaten egg. Pat potato mixture evenly into greased 10-in. pie plate to form crust, building up sides to

rim. Bake at 400° for 25 minutes or until crust just begins to brown. Remove from oven. (Crust may be prepared to this point, cooled, covered and refrigerated until ready to serve. To reheat, place in cold oven; set temperature to 350°. Heat for 10 minutes.) Sprinkle turkey ham, remaining onion and cheese in layers evenly over crust (crust should be hot when these ingredients are added). Set aside. In a small bowl, combine the milk, eggs, mustard and white pepper; mix well. Pour over crust ingredients. Place in oven; immediately reduce oven temperature to 350°. Bake for 30-35 minutes or until a knife inserted in center comes out clean. Let stand 5 minutes before cutting. **Yield:** 6 servings.

HOT TURKEY
TACO SALAD
Jean Bergin, Mishicot, Wisconsin

(PICTURED ON PAGE 8)

1 tablespoon vegetable oil
1 pound uncooked ground
    turkey
1 small green pepper, chopped
1 package taco seasoning mix,
    mild *or* hot
1 can (15-16 ounces) kidney
    beans, drained
1 can (6 ounces) ripe pitted
    olives, sliced
1 fresh tomato, chopped
1/2 cup taco sauce *or* salsa
1/4 cup Italian salad dressing
1/2 medium-sized head lettuce,
    shredded
1 package (8 ounces) nacho-
    flavored corn chips, crushed
1/2 to 3/4 cup shredded cheddar
    or Cojack cheese

Heat oil in a large skillet; add ground turkey, stirring until turkey browns. Add green pepper and seasoning mix (with amount of water called for on packet instructions). Cook for 10-15 minutes. Add beans, olives and tomato. Combine salsa/taco sauce and dressing; pour into the turkey mixture and heat. Just before serving, place the shredded lettuce and crushed chips on platter, fanning some whole chips around edge of dish. Spoon turkey mixture over chips and lettuce. Serve with the shredded cheese and additional salsa or taco sauce. **Yield:** 6 servings.

BARBECUED TURKEY
Holly Petersen, Hunter, North Dakota

(PICTURED ON PAGE 8)

1 fresh turkey (12 to 14
    pounds)
1 syringe (12cc), available from
    veterinarian or farm supply
    store
INJECTION SAUCE:
1/2 cup water
1 tablespoon salt
1-1/2 teaspoons garlic juice* *or*
    garlic salt
1-1/2 teaspoons Tabasco sauce
6 tablespoons lemon juice
BASTING SAUCE:
1/2 cup butter
1/2 clove garlic
2 teaspoons flour
1/3 cup water
3 tablespoons lemon juice
1-1/2 teaspoons sugar
1 teaspoon salt
1/2 teaspoon pepper
1/2 teaspoon poultry seasoning
1/8 teaspoon Tabasco sauce

*Garlic juice can be found in the seasonings section of many supermarkets. Combine injection sauce ingredients; fill syringe and inject into all meaty portions of turkey until skin is tight. (Inject slowly, withdrawing needle gradually to allow maximum juice retention.) Cover turkey loosely; refrigerate for several hours or overnight until time to grill. Place turkey on rotisserie or in shallow drip pan on top of grill. Use indirect heat method if cooking on a covered charcoal grill. Use low heat setting if cooking on a gas grill. While turkey cooks, prepare the basting sauce by melting butter in saucepan. Add the garlic; cook, stirring for several minutes. Stir in flour; cook until bubbly. Remove from heat; add the remaining ingredients. Return to heat; cook until mixture thickens and boils. Brush on turkey about 15 minutes before removing from grill. Check for doneness after 2 hours by inserting meat thermometer in thickest part of thigh, next to body (not resting on bone). Turkey is done when thermometer registers between 180° and 185°. (Our test turkey, about 11 lbs., was done in 2-1/2 hours. Time will vary with grill.) Let turkey stand for 15 minutes before carving. **Yield:** 20 servings.

GRILLED TURKEY STEAKS
Barbara Wellnitz, Ashby, Minnesota

(PICTURED ON PAGE 8)

2-1/2 to 3 pounds boneless uncooked turkey breast, cut into 1-1/2-inch-thick steaks

MARINADE:
1/4 cup vegetable oil
2 cloves garlic, minced
1-1/2 teaspoons oregano
2 tablespoons lemon juice
1/2 teaspoon salt
1/8 teaspoon fresh ground pepper

CASHEW BUTTER:
1/4 cup butter *or* margarine
2 teaspoons lemon juice
1/2 cup coarsely chopped cashews

Combine marinade ingredients; marinate steaks in refrigerator 2 hours or overnight. Cook on grill over medium heat about 10 minutes per side or until done—*do not overcook.* Heat cashew butter ingredients in microwave or on top of stove. Serve warm with steaks. **Yield:** 6-8 servings.

STIR-FRY TURKEY WITH WALNUTS
Terri Holmgren, Swanville, Minnesota

(PICTURED ON PAGE 9)

 This tasty dish uses less sugar, salt and fat. Recipe includes *Diabetic Exchanges.*

SAUCE:
3 tablespoons low-sodium soy sauce
2 teaspoons cornstarch
2 tablespoons dry sherry wine *or* apple juice
1 teaspoon grated fresh ginger root
1 teaspoon toasted sesame oil*, optional
1 teaspoon sugar
1/2 teaspoon salt
1/2 teaspoon crushed red pepper
2 tablespoons peanut oil *or* vegetable oil
2 green *or* red peppers, cut in 3/4-inch pieces
4 green onions, bias-sliced in 1-inch lengths
1 cup walnut halves
1-1/2 pounds uncooked turkey breast, skinned, cut in 1-inch cubes

*Toasted sesame oil can be found in the Oriental food section of many supermarkets. In small bowl, blend all sauce ingredients; set aside. Preheat wok over high heat; add oil. Stir-fry green peppers and onions in hot oil 2 minutes; remove from wok. Add walnuts to wok. Stir-fry 1-2 minutes or until golden brown; remove. Add more oil as needed. Add half of turkey. Stir-fry for 2 minutes or until browned on all sides; remove. Repeat with remaining turkey. Return all turkey to wok; stir in sauce. Stir, cooking until mixture thickens. Stir in the vegetables. Cover; cook for 1 minute. Stir in walnuts. Serve at once with hot cooked rice. **Yield:** 6 servings. **Diabetic Exchanges:** One serving equals 4 protein, 2 breads; also, 423 calories, 553 mg sodium, 59 mg cholesterol, 27 gm carbohydrate, 33 gm protein, 20 gm fat.

TURKEY SCALLOPINI
JoAnne Hill, Lisbon, Maryland

(PICTURED ON PAGE 9)

1/2 to 3/4 pound uncooked turkey cutlets (turkey breast slices)
1/2 cup flour, seasoned with salt and pepper
3 tablespoons butter, *divided*
2 tablespoons olive oil
1 small garlic clove, sliced thin
1/4 pound fresh mushrooms, sliced
1 to 2 tablespoons lemon juice
1/3 cup chicken broth
1/4 cup white wine *or* additional chicken broth

Pound turkey to 1/8-in thickness. Flour lightly, shaking off all excess. In skillet, melt *2 tablespoons* of butter, adding oil and garlic. Brown meat on both sides until golden brown, about 3 minutes. Place browned meat in ovenproof casserole dish. Add remaining butter and mushrooms to skillet and saute until mushrooms lose their crispness. Add to casserole. In a skillet, combine the lemon juice, broth and wine; stir and heat until mixture bubbles. Pour over casserole. Bake at 325° for about 30 minutes. (This recipe can be prepared in advance *up to baking*, refrigerated and popped into the oven when guests arrive.) **Yield:** 4 servings.

GRILLED TURKEY TENDERLOIN
Helen Miller, Teutopolis, Illinois

(PICTURED ON PAGE 9)

 This tasty dish uses less sugar, salt and fat. Recipe includes *Diabetic Exchanges.*

MARINADE:
1/4 cup low-sodium soy sauce
1/4 cup peanut oil
1/4 cup sherry wine *or* apple juice
2 tablespoons lemon juice
1/8 teaspoon black pepper
1/8 teaspoon garlic salt
2 tablespoons crushed onion
1/4 teaspoon ground ginger
1 pound uncooked turkey tenderloins, 3/4 to 1 inch thick

In a shallow pan, blend all marinade ingredients together. Add turkey, turning to coat both sides. Cover; marinate in refrigerator several hours or overnight, turning occasionally. Grill the tenderloins over hot coals, 8-10 minutes per side, depending on the thickness. Tenderloins are done when there is no pink in center—*do not overcook.* Serve in 1/4-in.-thick slices in toasted buns. **Yield:** 4 servings. **Diabetic Exchanges:** One serving equals 4 protein, 2 fats; also, 290 calories, 761 mg sodium, 59 mg cholesterol, 4 gm carbohydrate, 27 gm protein, 16 gm fat.

TASTY GROUND TURKEY: Fresh, uncooked ground turkey makes an interesting substitute in dishes that use ground beef. Try it for Stroganoff, "Sloppy Toms", spaghetti sauce, lasagna, tacos, enchiladas, casseroles and as all or part of the meat in meat loaf. Season sparingly, since ground turkey does accept seasoning more readily than do other ground meats.

● When a recipe calls for turkey sausage and none is available, substitute plain ground turkey and add fennel seed, garlic, oregano and basil.

● For a delicious hamburger variation, mix equal parts ground turkey and ground beef.

DAY-AFTER TURKEY PIE
Kay Smith, Gooding, Idaho

(PICTURED ON PAGE 9)

CRUST:
- 1-1/2 cups flour
- 1-1/2 teaspoons baking powder
- 3/4 teaspoon salt
- 1/2 cup shortening
- 6 tablespoons hot water
- 1 egg, *divided*
- 2 teaspoons lemon juice

FILLING:
- 1-1/2 cups cold cooked turkey, cut up
- 1 cup turkey dressing, crumbled
- 1-1/2 cups turkey gravy (may extend with undiluted mushroom soup)
- 1 cup celery, diced
- 2 tablespoons butter, optional

For crust, combine flour, baking powder and salt; cut in the shortening. Combine water, beaten egg yolk and lemon juice; stir in until crust mixture forms a ball. Divide into two portions; roll out each to fit 9-in. pie pan or 8-in. square baking dish. Combine all filling ingredients *except butter* and place in a pastry-lined dish. Dot with butter, if desired. Cover with top crust. Cut in steam vents; brush with reserved beaten egg white. Bake at 425° for 30 minutes. **Yield:** 6 servings.

TURKEY ENCHILADAS
Jo Groth, Plainfield, Iowa

(PICTURED ON PAGE 10)

- 1/2 cup chopped onions
- 1 can (4 ounces) green chilies, drained *or* green peppers, *divided*
- 3 tablespoons butter, *divided*
- 1/3 cup taco sauce
- 1 cup dairy sour cream, *divided*
- 1/8 teaspoon chili powder
- 2-1/2 cups cooked cubed turkey
- 2 cups shredded cheddar cheese, *divided*
- 10 flour tortillas
- 2 tablespoons flour
- 1 cup chicken *or* turkey broth
- 1/2 cup chopped fresh tomato

In a glass bowl, combine the onions, *2 tablespoons* chilies *or* peppers and *1 tablespoon* butter. Microwave (MW) on HIGH for 1 minutes. Add taco sauce,

1/4 cup sour cream and chili powder. Stir in turkey and *1/2 cup* cheese. Divide the mixture among tortillas. Roll tortillas; place seam side down in 13-in. x 9-in. x 2-in. baking dish. MW remaining 2 tablespoons butter until melted. Blend in flour, then slowly stir in broth. MW on HIGH 3-4 minutes until thickened, stirring every minute. Stir in the remaining sour cream and remaining chilies *or* peppers. Pour over enchiladas. MW enchiladas on MEDIUM for 6-8 minutes. Sprinkle with remaining cheese and tomatoes. MW at MEDIUM until all the cheese is melted. **Conventional Method:** Combine filling ingredients; fill tortillas. Place in greased baking dish and bake 45 minutes at 325°. Sprinkle cheese and tomatoes over top. Return to oven until cheese is melted. **Yield:** 8-10 servings.

TURKEY PICCATA
Perlene Hoekema, Lynden, Washington

(PICTURED ON PAGE 10)

- 2 eggs
- 2 tablespoons milk
- 3-1/2 cups fresh bread crumbs (about 8 slices processed in food processor *or* blender)
- 2 packages (14-16 ounces *each*) uncooked turkey cutlets *or* half of a 5-pound to 6-pound frozen turkey breast, thawed and cut in 1/4-inch-thick slices
- About 3/4 cup butter *or* margarine
- 2 large lemons, *divided*
- 1-1/2 cups water
- 2 teaspoons chicken-flavor bouillon
- 1/2 teaspoon salt
- Parsley sprigs

Beat eggs with milk in shallow dish until well blended. Place bread crumbs on waxed paper. Dip cutlets in egg mixture then in crumbs, coating both sides. Melt the butter *or* margarine, as needed, in a 12-in. skillet over a medium high heat. Brown turkey cutlets, 4-6 at a time, on both sides. Remove to a plate; keep warm. Reduce heat to low. Squeeze juice of 1 lemon (about 1/4 cup) into pan drippings in skillet; stir in water, bouillon to skillet; cover and simmer 15 minutes. Thinly slice remaining lemon. To serve, arrange cutlets on large warm platter and garnish with lemon slices. Pour remaining sauce over cutlets; sprinkle with parsley. **Yield:** 8 servings.

TANGY TURKEY SALAD
Merridy Kienitz, Blue Earth, Minnesota

(PICTURED ON PAGE 10)

✓ This tasty dish uses less sugar, salt and fat. Recipe includes *Diabetic Exchanges*.

DRESSING:
- 1/2 cup reduced calorie creamy salad dressing
- 1/4 cup dairy sour cream
- 1 tablespoon fresh chives
- 1 tablespoon sugar
- 1 teaspoon ground ginger
- 1/2 teaspoon grated lemon rind
- 1 tablespoon fresh lemon juice
- 1/4 teaspoon salt

SALAD:
- 2 to 3 cups cubed cooked white turkey
- 1 cup seedless green grapes, halved if desired
- 1 cup sliced celery
- 1 cup drained pineapple chunks, halved if desired
- Curly leaf lettuce
- 4 cantaloupe rings, peeled and seeded, cut 3/4 inch thick
- 1/2 cup toasted pecans

Combine all dressing ingredients; mix well. Refrigerate. Prepare salad ingredients and mix lightly with dressing. Cover individual luncheon plates with base of lettuce and fill center with salad. Garnish with pecans. **Yield:** 4 servings. **Diabetic Exchanges:** One serving equals 3-1/2 protein, 2 breads, 2 fats; also, 403 calories, 389 mg sodium, 86 mg cholesterol, 29 gm carbohydrate, 34 gm protein, 17 gm fat.

TURKEY TIPS: The best way to roast a turkey is in a shallow pan with a "tent" of heavy aluminum foil over it. Roast at 325 degrees for about 15 to 20 minutes per pound. After roasting, let the turkey stand for 15-20 minutes before carving.

● To remove a large, hot roasted turkey from the pan, slip on a pair of insulated oven mitts and cover them with plastic bags. The bird will lift safely and easily to the cutting board.

● Save the last-minute rush when you're serving turkey and stuffing to a large group! Roast the turkey the day before, carve it, and store the meat and stuffing—separately—in the refrigerator. To reheat, place in wire salad baskets in an improvised steamer. (Place an empty tincan in the bottom of a large kettle and set basket on top of can; add enough water to steam. Cover; steam for 30 minutes.

WILLIAMSBURG INN TURKEY SOUP
Muriel Lerdal, Humboldt, Iowa

(PICTURED ON PAGE 10)

1 turkey carcass
4 quarts water
3 large onions, chopped fine
3 stalks celery, chopped fine
2 large carrots, chopped fine
1/4 cup uncooked long grain rice
1 cup butter *or* margarine
1-1/2 cups flour
1 pint half-and-half
3 cups diced cooked turkey
1/2 teaspoon poultry seasoning, if desired
Salt, pepper to taste

In large kettle, cook turkey carcass with water to make 3 qts. stock. Remove bones; reserve meat for soup. Strain stock; set aside. In saucepan, combine onions, celery, carrots, rice and 1 qt. of the stock. Cook for 20 minutes; set aside. In a large soup kettle, melt butter *or* margarine. Blend in flour and heat until bubbly. Add half-and-half and remaining 2 qts. stock to butter/flour mixture; cook and stir until bubbly. Stir in the reserved vegetable mixture, turkey and seasonings to taste. Heat slowly to serving temperature. **Yield:** 4 to 4-1/2 qts. (This soup freezes well.)

TURKEY A LA QUEEN
Martha Kaup, Defiance, Ohio

6 slices white bread, crusts trimmed
2 tablespoons melted butter, *divided*
1/4 cup slivered almonds
4 tablespoons butter
2 tablespoons flour
Dash black pepper
1 teaspoon salt
1/8 teaspoon paprika
1-1/2 cups half-and-half *or* evaporated milk
1 egg yolk, beaten
2 cups diced cooked turkey
1-1/2 cups seedless grapes

To make toast cups, brush trimmed bread slices lightly on one side with part of the melted butter. Gently push each slice, buttered side down, into large muffin tins, leaving the corners showing at top. Bake at 375° for 8-10 minutes or until corners are browned. Remove from oven; let cool in muffin tins. To prepare filling, saute almonds

in remaining melted butter (about 2 teaspoons) until light golden brown; set aside. In heavy saucepan, melt butter. Next add flour, pepper, salt and paprika, stirring until smooth. Slowly add half-and-half/milk. Pour a small amount of sauce over beaten egg yolk, stirring to blend. Return yolk mixture to remaining sauce. Cook and stir until thick. Add turkey and grapes. Heat. Spoon into toast cups. Garnish with reserved almonds. **Yield:** 6 servings.

TURKEY/WILD RICE CASSEROLE
Patty Nelson, Clear Lake, Wisconsin

1 box long grain/wild rice mix, prepared according to instructions on the package
2 packages (10 ounces *each*) frozen broccoli, thawed and drained
6 cups leftover cubed turkey
SAUCE:
1/2 cup creamy salad dressing *or* mayonnaise
2 cans (10-3/4 ounces *each*) cream of chicken soup
4 ounces water chestnuts, sliced and drained
1/2 teaspoon lemon juice
1 cup grated cheddar cheese

Spread cooked wild rice mixture over bottom of greased 13-in. x 9-in. x 2-in. baking pan. Place broccoli spears on top of rice; add cubed turkey. Combine sauce ingredients except cheese; spread over top of casserole. Sprinkle cheese over all. Bake at 350° for 55 minutes or MW on HIGH for 12 minutes or until casserole is heated through. **Yield:** 8 servings.

SMOKED TURKEY SOUP: The carcass and leftover meat from a 10-lb. to 14-lb. smoked grilled turkey makes a wonderful base for a bean soup. For the broth, cover the carcass with 4 to 6 quarts of water and add 2 cups coarsely chopped onion, 6 cups chopped celery stems (with leaves), 4 peeled and shredded carrots, 4 to 6 cloves chopped garlic, 2 tablespoons of seasoning/herb mixture and salt to taste. Simmer for 2 hours. Remove the bones; reserve meat. Cool stock; skim fat from top. Add about 2 lbs. of soaked Navy beans to stock; simmer until the beans are halfway cooked. Add reserved turkey meat; cook until the beans are tender.

BEST-OF-THE-DINNER SANDWICHES
Freda Holmes, Oklahoma City, Oklahoma

1 English muffin *per person served*
Chili sauce
Creamy salad dressing *or* mayonnaise
Leftover sliced turkey
Leftover turkey dressing
Leftover cranberry sauce
Cheddar, American or Swiss cheese slices
Cooked, crumbled bacon

Lightly toast muffins in 400° oven on ungreased cookie sheet; remove from oven. Combine one part chili sauce with two parts salad dressing/mayonnaise; spread on each of muffin halves. Layer turkey, thin layer of stuffing, thin layer of cranberry sauce and slice of cheese on bottom halves of muffins; reserve tops. Place filled muffin bottoms in oven for 10 minutes or until cheese melts. (May also microwave.) Remove from oven; top with bacon and reserved muffin halves.

REUBEN CASSEROLE
Susan Dukes, Sawyer Air Force Base, Michigan

1 can (1 pound) sauerkraut, drained
1 teaspoon caraway seed
2 cups (8 ounces) shredded Monterey Jack cheese, *divided*
1/2 cup Thousand Island dressing
1 cup cubed turkey pastrami *or* turkey ham
4 thick slices rye bread, cut in 1/2-inch cubes
1/3 cup melted butter
2 tablespoons chopped fresh parsley

Place drained sauerkraut loosely in a 10-in. glass pie plate. Sprinkle with caraway seed, 1 cup of cheese, dressing, turkey and the remaining cheese. Toss bread cubes with melted butter; sprinkle over cheese. Microwave on MEDIUM for about 10 minutes or until cheese is heated through. Garnish with chopped parsley. **Yield:** 6 servings of 1 cup each.

16

STUFFING STUFF: To make making stuffing easy, cook the giblets until done, cool, and chop with celery and onion in a food processor until the desired texture.

● A 1-lb. loaf of bread will make up about 8 cups of loosely packed crumbs for stuffing. Allow 1 cup of stuffing for each pound of turkey.

SALSA
Elizabeth Erro Hvolboll, Goleta, California

4 cans (8 ounces each) tomato sauce
1/2 to 1 medium onion, *chopped fine*
1/2 to 1 can (4 ounces) *chopped* green chilies
4 to 6 cloves garlic, *crushed*
2 tablespoons olive oil
Juice of 1/2 lemon
1 can (6 ounces) black olives, *drained*

Combine all ingredients; chill. Serve as steak sauce or dip for corn chips. **Yield:** About 6 cups.

CHEESY MEAT LOAF
Diane Mork, Swisher, Iowa

1-1/2 pounds lean ground beef
1 egg
3/4 cup cracker crumbs
2 tablespoons minced onion
1 teaspoon salt
1/8 to 1/4 teaspoon oregano
1/2 teaspoon pepper
1 can (8 ounces) tomato sauce, *divided*
2 cups shredded mozzarella *or* cheddar cheese *or* combination of both
1/4 teaspoon Italian seasoning

Combine beef, egg, crumbs, onion, salt, oregano, pepper and 1/3 can tomato sauce. Mix well. Shape into flat rectangle about 8 x 12 in. on waxed paper. Pat or roll to even thickness, about 1/4 in. Sprinkle cheese evenly over meat; roll up like jelly roll, pressing ends to seal. Place roll in 9 x 12-in glass baking dish. Pour remaining tomato sauce mixed with Italian seasoning over top. Cover with waxed paper; microwave 12-15 minutes on HIGH. Let stand at least 10 minutes before serving. **Yield:** 6-8 servings. **Conventional method:** Bake at 350° for 1 hour.

HERB VINEGARS
Glacier Bay Country Inn
Gustavus, Alaska

3-1/2 cups white vinegar *or* wine vinegar
Seasonings/herbs of choice

Scald a 1-quart bottle with a tight-fitting top; let dry completely. Place desired herb/seasonings in bottle. Heat vinegar in medium saucepan just to boiling. Let cool slightly; pour into bottle. Let cool. Seal tightly. Let stand in dark place at room temperature for 2-3 weeks, shaking occasionally. Strain and rebottle with sprigs of fresh herbs. **Yield:** About 1 quart.
   Tarragon: Use 1 cup fresh tarragon, 2 cloves garlic.
   Dill: Use about 1 cup dill.
   Garlic: Use 8 peeled, whole cloves of garlic.
   Chive: Use 2 cups chives.

TURKEY FRUIT SALAD
Lucy Dalton, Washburn, Missouri

4 cups chopped cooked turkey
1 cup (8-1/2 ounces) canned pineapple tidbits
1 cup seedless grapes
1 cup chopped, unpeeled apple
1 cup chopped walnuts
1 cup mayonnaise, more or less as desired

Toss all ingredients together lightly; chill and serve. **Yield:** 6 servings.

CHEESE RICE SOUFFLE
Martha Patch, Winter Gardens, Florida

2 eggs, *separated*
1 tablespoon butter, *melted*
1 cup milk
1 cup grated sharp cheddar cheese
2 cups cooked long grain rice
1/4 teaspoon paprika
8 drops Tabasco sauce
Salt to taste, if desired

Beat egg yolks until thick. Combine with butter, milk, cheese, rice and seasonings. Mix well. Beat egg whites until stiff and fold into egg yolk mixture. Pour into buttered 2-qt. baking dish and bake at 350° for 25-30 minutes. Serve immediately. **Yield:** 6-8 servings.

PORK CHOPS AND DRESSING
Amy Kraemer, Glencoe, Minnesota

4 loin pork chops, 1/2 inch thick
Kitchen Bouquet
3 cups herb-seasoned croutons
1/4 cup diced onion
1/4 cup melted butter
1 egg, slightly beaten
1/4 cup water
1 can (10-3/4 ounces) cream of mushroom soup
1/3 cup milk

Brush both sides of chops with Kitchen Bouquet; set aside. Combine croutons, onion, butter and egg mixed with 1/4 cup water. Spread in bottom of 8- x 12-in. glass baking dish. Place chops on dressing. Cover with plastic wrap; microwave on HIGH for 5 minutes. Remove wrap carefully; turn chops. Pour soup mixed with milk over all. Re-cover and microwave on 70% POWER for 10 minutes. Let stand for at least 5 minutes, covered, before serving. **Yield:** 4 servings. **Conventional method:** Bake at 350° for 1 hour. Omit plastic wrap; cover with foil.

EASY CHICKEN DIVAN CASSEROLE
Judy Merchant, Port Washington, Wisconsin

2 packages (10 ounces each) frozen broccoli, cut up, cooked and drained
2 cups cooked cubed chicken (white meat preferred)
2 cans (10-3/4 ounces each) *undiluted* cream of chicken soup
1 cup mayonnaise
1 teaspoon to 1 tablespoon fresh lemon juice
1/2 teaspoon curry powder
TOPPING
1/2 cup shredded cheddar cheese
1/2 cup soft bread crumbs
1 tablespoon butter

Combine cooked broccoli and chicken in bottom of greased 12-in. x 9-in. x 2-in. baking pan. Set aside. Combine soup, mayonnaise, lemon juice and curry powder in a bowl; pour over chicken/broccoli. Mix cheese and bread crumbs with butter, sprinkle over top of casserole. Bake at 350° for 30 minutes. **Yield:** 12 servings.

COUNTRY INNS

Rancho De Chimayo

P.O. Box 11, Chimayo, New Mexico 87522

Phone: 1-505/351-2222

Directions: From Santa Fe, take Highway 285 north for 12 miles to Pojoaque, turn right for 8 miles on State Road 503 toward Nambe, take a sharp left on State Road 520 toward Chimayo for 3 miles.

Owners: Florence and Laura Jaramillo

Schedule: Open Feb. through Dec.

Accommodations and Rates: Seven rooms with private baths and adobe fireplaces, $49 to $76. Includes continental breakfast for two. $10 each additional person in room. Children over age 3 welcome. No pets.

Spicy but not too hot describes the fine New Mexican food served at the Restaurante Rancho de Chimayo. Their dishes—prepared from recipes which have been in the family for years —include the "Combinacion Picante" featuring *carne adovada* (marinated pork), tamale, enchilada, beans and posole or the "Platon Especial" which includes guacamole, enchilada, tamale, taco and *torta de huevo* (beef, cheese and green chili omelet).

Puffy sopaipillas—light, delicious fried dough triangles—are served with honey to accompany the meals.

Desserts include smooth flan and natilla, a creamy vanilla milk pudding with meringue and cinnamon topping.

NATILLA

4 cups milk
8 eggs, separated
3 tablespoons cornstarch
3 tablespoons milk
2 cups sugar
1/4 teaspoon vanilla

Warm milk in a double boiler until nearly boiling. Add beaten egg yolks. Dissolve cornstarch in 3 tablespoons milk, stir into mixture. Add sugar and vanilla. Cook until thickened—2 to 5 minutes. Pour pudding into bowl or individual serving dishes. Beat egg whites with one teaspoon sugar until stiff. Place beaten egg whites in islands on top of pudding; sprinkle with cinnamon. **Yield:** 8 servings.

GUACAMOLE

4 medium avocados
1/2 cup canned green chiles, chopped
1/2 fresh tomato, seeded and chopped
2 teaspoons finely chopped onions
2 teaspoons mayonnaise
1/2 teaspoon salt
1/4 teaspoon garlic salt
1/4 teaspoon white pepper
1/2 teaspoon Worcestershire sauce *or* lemon juice

Peel and seed avocados, add remaining ingredients, and mash with potato masher until of desired smoothness. Serve as a dip with tortilla chips. **Yield:** 5 cups.

CARNE ADOVADA

6 boned, tenderized pork chops, cut in cubes

CHILE CARIBE SAUCE:
1/2 pound whole chile pods
1/2 teaspoon salt
1/2 teaspoon finely chopped onions
1/4 teaspoon white pepper
1/2 teaspoon oregano
1/4 teaspoon Worcestershire sauce

Wash whole red chile pods, removing stem and seeds. Roast in 350° oven about 3 to 5 minutes, watching closely to keep them from burning. Break up peppers into a bowl and add remaining seasonings. Blend 1/4 of the chile mixture with 3/4 cup water, repeating until all the mixture is blended and you have about a quart of sauce. (Or use dried pepper pods. Remove stem and seeds, break up into bowl and cover with boiling water until light red-orange and spongy. Blend mixture with remaining seasonings). Boil sauce over medium heat for 20 minutes. Pour sauce over meat and bake in a 350° oven for one hour. **Yield:** 6 servings.

SOPAIPILLAS

2 cups flour
1-1/2 teaspoons salt
1/2 teaspoon baking powder
1-1/2 teaspoons sugar (optional)
1-1/2 teaspoons shortening
1/2 to 2/3 cup warm water as needed
1 tablespoon evaporated milk
Shortening for frying

Combine flour, salt, baking powder and sugar. Cut in 1-1/2 teaspoons shortening. Add water and milk; work into dough. Divide the dough into 12 balls. Roll each to 1/4-inch thick, cut in half and fry in melted shortening at 450°. **Yield:** 24 sopaipillas.

CRUSTY MEXICAN BEAN BAKE

Sharon Schmidt, Vanderhoof, BC

CRUST:
1/2 cup all-purpose flour
1/2 teaspoon salt
1/2 teaspoon baking powder
2 tablespoons shortening
1/2 cup sour cream *or* yogurt (add 2 more tablespoons flour if using yogurt)
1 egg, beaten

FILLING:
3/4 pound ground beef
1/2 cup chopped onion
1 teaspoon salt
2 teaspoons chili powder
3/4 cup (6 ounces) tomato paste
1/2 teaspoon Tabasco sauce
2 cups *undrained*, cooked kidney beans

TOPPING:
1/2 cup grated cheese
1/2 cup shredded lettuce
1 cup chopped fresh tomatoes

Stir together crust ingredients (may be slightly lumpy). Spread thinly with back of spoon on bottom and sides of shallow greased 2-qt. baking pan. Set aside. Brown beef and onion in skillet; drain fat. Add remaining filling ingredients; place in crust. Bake at 350° for 30 minutes. Remove from oven. Sprinkle topping ingredients on top or serve as accompaniments. **Yield:** 10 servings. (Crust can be made ahead and stored in refrigerator.)

BEST COOK

Did you ever wonder whether prize-winning cooks save their best efforts for contests and serve "just average" dishes to their family? Well, that's certainly not true of Gloria Piantek, nominated as "Best Cook in the Country" by her husband, Thomas.

"Gloria's entered recipe contests as a hobby since 1968," he relates. "I used to tease her about it—until she started winning them regularly!

"She has a real talent for creating interesting, original dishes...but not just for contests. Every meal that she serves at home is a real winner, too."

When company comes, Gloria's meals make them feel right at home, even if home's half a world away!

"Once we had a visitor from Japan," Thomas wrote. "Gloria went to work in her country kitchen on an All-American meal with Oriental touches. Afterward, our friend said it was the best meal he'd ever tasted in the United States!"

Closer to home, Gloria—who's a special education teacher—uses her cooking skills to help students. "There was a boy who needed help with reading, so Gloria brought him home to our kitchen and tied a big apron on him," Thomas relates. "In no time, he was helping by reading directions and writing down ingredients! To Gloria, cooking is a loving, sharing and learning experience."

SIDEWINDERS SUCCOTASH SALAD

    4 green onions, sliced, about
      1/3 cup
1-1/2 cups canned *or* cooked whole
      kernel corn, drained
    1 can (16 ounces) garbanzo
      beans, drained
    1 cup coarsely chopped
      zucchini
    1 can (4 ounces) mild *or*
      medium chopped green
      chilies
  1/2 cup chopped seeded
      tomatoes
  1/2 cup mayonnaise *or* salad
      dressing
    1 clove garlic, minced
    1 tablespoon brown sugar
  1/2 teaspoon dry mustard
  1/4 teaspoon salt *or* as desired
  1/8 teaspoon pepper *or* as
      desired
Garnish of bibb lettuce leaves

In large bowl, combine onions, corn, garbanzo beans, zucchini, chilies and tomatoes. Set aside. In small bowl, combine mayonnaise/salad dressing, garlic, brown sugar, dry mustard, salt and pepper. Stir together until well mixed. Toss the dressing with vegetables until well coated. Chill in refrigerator at least 1 hour or until serving time. Garnish bowl with fresh lettuce leaves. **Yield:** 6-8 servings.

LICKETY SPLIT LEMON REFRIGERATOR CAKE

    1 package (2 layer size)
      lemon cake mix
    2 packages (3 ounces *each*)
      lemon-flavored gelatin mix
1-1/2 cups boiling water
1-1/2 cups lemon/lime soda
    1 package (3-1/2 ounces)
      lemon *instant* pudding
1-1/3 cups cold milk
    1 cup whipping cream,
      whipped

Prepare and bake cake in 13-in. x 9-in. x 2-in. pan according to package directions. Meanwhile, dissolve gelatin in hot water; then gently mix in lemon/lime soda. Chill in refrigerator until cake is baked. While cake is hot, with a fork, punch holes in cake and spoon cool gelatin mixture over cake. Refrigerate. In bowl, beat together lemon pudding and milk until thickened. Fold in whipped cream. Spread over top of cake. Chill completely. Cut into squares to serve. Garnish with fresh lemon/lime slices and mint leaves. **Yield:** 18-20 servings.

ARCTIC FUDGE BARS

    6 ounces white chocolate
    1 package (8 ounces) cream
      cheese, softened
  1/2 cup granulated sugar
    1 egg
    1 package (1 ounce) *premelted*
      unsweetened chocolate
  1/4 cup butter *or* margarine,
      softened
    1 cup granulated sugar
    4 eggs
  1/2 teaspoon vanilla flavoring
  1/4 teaspoon almond flavoring
    1 cup all-purpose flour
  1/2 teaspoon baking powder
  1/4 teaspoon salt

Place white chocolate in microwave dish, cook on HIGH 1-1/2 minutes or until melted, stirring every 30 seconds. Set aside to cool. In small bowl, combine cream cheese, sugar and egg until mixture is smooth. Add unsweetened chocolate, mixing until uniform in color; set aside. In mixing bowl, mix the butter and sugar to combine; beat in eggs until foamy. Add the flavorings and white chocolate; beat until smooth. Stir in flour, baking powder and salt. Spread the white chocolate batter in greased 13-in. x 9-in. x 2-in baking pan. Place spoonfuls of chocolate cheese over top of batter. Swirl a knife through to marbleize slightly. Bake at 350° for 35 to 40 minutes or until done. Cool. Chill in refrigerator. Cut into bars to serve. **Yield:** 24 bars.

POTATO POINTERS: Potatoes soaked in salt water for 20 minutes before baking will bake more rapidly.

● Let raw potatoes stand in cold water for at least 30 minutes before frying to improve the crispness of French fries.

● A few drops of lemon juice in the water will whiten boiled potatoes.

avor the flavors of the Deep South with this tasty selection of "down-home" dishes! These recipes simmer with a Southern accent reminiscent of the lush gardens of Mississippi...the ripe orchards of Georgia...the fertile fields of Louisiana...the henhouses of North Carolina...and the smokehouses of Virginia. They're sure to satisfy in your home—whatever state it's in!

Sample simple but flavorful fare like Grandmother's Chicken 'n' Dumplings and hearty, regional favorites like Black Bean Soup. Serve side dishes such as light, corn-rich Spoon Bread...tender, tasty Turnip Greens...or orange-sauced Praline/Yam Casserole.

Company's coming! Dish up some Southern-style hospitality with succulent Herb-Seasoned Roast Pork, sweet Stuffed Vidalia Onions or Crab and Country Ham Pasta—farm-fresh fare that's fancy enough to serve the city cousins!

The South's as close as your kitchen when you cook up these tasty treats. Enjoy 'em all, y'all!

SOUTHERN STARS: Clockwise from lower left—**Southern Turnip Greens,** Jennie Lee Hyde, Senatobia, Mississippi (Pg. 27); **Spoon Bread,** Lillie Lowery, Kennesaw, Georgia (Pg. 27); **Herb-Seasoned Pork Roast,** Carole Boyer, Converse, Indiana (Pg. 27); **Grandmother's Chicken 'n' Dumplings,** Cynthia Carroll, Cary, North Carolina (Pg. 28); **Black Bean Soup,** Mickey and Don Ertel, Barefoot Bay, Florida (Pg. 28); **Praline/Yam Casserole,** Alice Mathews, Alexandria, Louisiana (Pg. 28); **Stuffed Vidalia Onions,** Suzanne McKinley, Lyons, Georgia (Pg. 28); **Crab and Country Ham Pasta,** Julia Wilcox, Williamsburg, Virginia (Pg. 27).

"You don't have to be a "Southern Belle" to bake up some scrumptious Southern desserts! Just try one of these family favorites...and count on serving seconds.

No Southern supper would be complete without a sweet, simple dessert of Banana Pudding, Texas Pecan Pie, Fresh Blackberry Cobbler or tender Banana Spice Cake. Top off your Southern "taste tour" in style—with one or more of these delicious Dixie desserts!

Linens from Percy's Inc., Milwaukee, Wisconsin.

SWEET SOMETHINGS: Top to bottom —**Banana Pudding,** Doris Clayton, Germantown, Tennessee; **Banana Spice Cake,** Meredith Barrett, Dalton, Georgia; **Texas Pecan Pie,** Helen Suter, Rosenberg, Texas; **Blackberry Cobbler,** Trudy Cinque, Waynesville, North Carolina. (All recipes can be found on Page 29.)

Recipes from Lois Enger, Colorado Springs, Colorado

MEALS IN MINUTES

HERE'S A TIMELY taste treat that's perfect for an informal brunch or speedy supper. "Texas toast" is perfectly suited for making this quick, crunchy French toast, but any thick-sliced fresh bread will do. The corn flake crumbs make it different—and delicious!

You can top the toast with ordinary syrup, but after you taste this home-made cinnamon syrup, we don't think you'll want to. Serve Canadian bacon, sausage or bacon on the side...add fresh fruit cups or a fruit "smoothie" to fill out the menu...and you have a satisfying meal in less than half an hour!

CRUMB-TOPPED BAKED FRENCH TOAST

- 2 eggs, well beaten
- 1/2 cup milk
- 1/2 teaspoon salt
- 1/2 teaspoon vanilla
- 6 slices "Texas toast" or other thick-sliced bread
- 1 cup corn flake crumbs
- 1/4 cup butter, melted

CINNAMON SYRUP:

- 1-1/3 cups sugar
- 1/3 cup water
- 2/3 cup white corn syrup
- 1 teaspoon ground cinnamon
- 1 can (5 ounces) evaporated milk
- 1/2 teaspoon almond flavoring
- 1/2 teaspoon burnt sugar flavoring (optional)
- 1 tablespoon butter

Combine eggs, milk, salt and vanilla; mix well. Dip bread slices into egg mixture; coat both sides with crumbs. Place on well-greased cookie sheet. Drizzle melted butter over crumb-coated bread. Bake at 450° for 10 minutes. To make syrup, combine sugar, water, corn syrup and cinnamon in saucepan. Bring to boil; cook 2 minutes. Remove from heat; add milk, flavoring(s) and butter. Serve syrup warm with toast. **Yield:** 4 servings.

FRESH FRUIT CUPS

- 2 bananas, peeled and sliced
- 1 orange, peeled and cut in small pieces
- 2 red apples, washed, cored and cut in bite-sized pieces
- 1 kiwi fruit, peeled and cut in bite-sized pieces

Combine all ingredients and fold together gently. **Yield:** 4 servings.

MORNING MAGIC: For deliciously different scrambled eggs, add one spoonful of instant chicken broth and 2 half-shells of water to 6 beaten eggs. Cook as usual.

● Vary the flavor of French toast by using raisin/cinnamon bread instead of plain white bread.

For another fruity recipe on the run, try this refreshing "smoothie":

STRAWBERRY BANANA COOLER

Deanna House, Portage, Michigan

- 2 cups unsweetened orange juice
- 1/2 cup whole frozen strawberries
- 1 large banana, sliced
- 2 to 4 ice cubes

Combine all ingredients in a blender container. Cover tightly; blend until smooth and serve immediately. **Yield:** 3 to 4 servings.

Our old-time stove is chockful of breakfast treats—from muffins to strata and French toast to pizza! Tried and true, or trendy and new, this breakfast bonanza will really open your eyes!

BOUNTIFUL BREAKFASTS: Clockwise from lower left—**Coffee Cake Wheels,** Sue Pipkin, Baxter Springs, Kansas (Pg. 30); **Oven French Toast with Nut Topping,** Donna Justin, Sparta, Wisconsin (Pg. 30); **Hot Fruit Compote,** Jean Vaeraid, Huxley, Iowa (Pg. 30); **Spinach Quiche,** Lois Dethloff, Amboy, Minnesota (Pg. 31); **Lemon Yogurt Muffins,** Bev Neuenschwander, Dalton, Ohio (Pg. 31); **Chili Cheese Strata,** Shirley Smith, Anaheim, California (Pg. 31); **Oatmeal Waffles,** Marna Heitz, Farley, Iowa (Pg. 31); **Breakfast Pizza,** Wilma Richey, Lead Hill, Arkansas (Pg. 30).

Hearty breakfasts—there's no better way to begin a country day!

Your family will be glad for the good start these recipes give them. And you'll appreciate a handy aspect of these dishes—many of them can be made the night before!

These breakfasts satisfy assorted tastes to make the first meal of the day a "seconds, please" favorite.

RISE AND SHINE! Top to bottom—**Southern Plantation Corn Bread,** Beverly Plymell, Keytesville, Missouri; **Quiche Italiano,** Caryn Wiggins, Columbus, Indiana; **Scrambled Egg Casserole,** Mary Anne McWhirter, Pearland, Texas; **Buttermilk Cranberry Muffins,** Jane Yunker, Rochester, New York. (All recipes can be found on Page 32.)

HERB-SEASONED PORK ROAST
Carole Boyer, Converse, Indiana

(PICTURED ON PAGE 20)

1 teaspoon fennel
2 teaspoons salt
1/4 teaspoon pepper
1/2 teaspoon oregano
1/2 teaspoon crushed bay leaves
1/8 teaspoon ground nutmeg
1/8 teaspoon ground cloves
2 teaspoons chopped parsley
1 teaspoon minced onion
1 clove garlic, crushed or 1/4 teaspoon garlic powder
1 pork shoulder roast (6 to 8 pounds)

Combine all spices and herbs. Make slits 1/2 in. deep at 1-in. intervals in roast and rub spice mixture into slits and over roast surface. Place roast in covered pan in 2 in. of water; insert meat thermometer in center of roast. Bake at 350° for 1-1/2 to 2 hours or until thermometer registers 160°. **Yield:** 10-12 servings.

CRAB AND COUNTRY HAM PASTA
Julia Wilcox, WIlliamsburg, Virginia

(PICTURED ON PAGE 20)

1 pound fresh pasta (fettuccine is best)

SAUCE:
2 tablespoons butter
2 tablespoons flour
3/4 cup milk
3/4 cup light cream or half-and-half
3 tablespoons Parmesan cheese
2 tablespoons dry sherry, optional
1/4 teaspoon cayenne pepper, or to taste
Salt
Pepper
1 tablespoon vegetable oil
1/4 pound cooked country ham, cut in julienne strips*
1 bunch green onions, chopped
1/2 pound crab meat, all shell removed
1 red pepper, cut in julienne strips

(*Use an authentic, salt-cured country ham.) Cook pasta according to package directions; keep warm. Melt butter over low heat in skillet; add flour and blend with whisk to form a roux. Cook over medium heat for 2 minutes (do not burn). Remove from heat; whisk in milk and cream. Return to heat; add cheese, sherry (if desired), cayenne pepper and salt and pepper. If mixture becomes too thick, add more milk and cream. Keep warm. In another skillet, saute ham and onions in vegetable oil for 2 minutes over medium heat. Add crab and pepper strips; saute for 1 minute. Stir crab mixture into sauce. Serve over hot, drained pasta as an appetizer or as a main dish. **Yield:** 4-8 servings.

SOUTHERN TURNIP GREENS
Jennie Lee Hyde, Senatobia, Mississippi

(PICTURED ON PAGE 20)

2 cups cooked, chopped turnip greens or 1 pound fresh greens
Salt
Pepper
1 teaspoon sugar
2 teaspoons vinegar
1 teaspoon horseradish sauce
1/2 cup mayonnaise
5 ounces cream of mushroom soup (1/2 of 10-3/4-ounce can), undiluted
2 eggs, beaten
1/2 cup soft bread crumbs
1/2 cup grated cheddar cheese
Bacon bits, if desired

Stem and wash fresh greens; place in water in large kettle. Bring to boil; reduce heat and cook until tender. Grind in food processor and measure 2 cups for recipe. (Substitute cooked, frozen greens.) Combine greens with salt, pepper, sugar, vinegar, horseradish sauce, mayonnaise, soup and eggs. Mix well; place in 8-in. x 8-in. casserole dish. Sprinkle crumbs, cheese and bacon bits on top. Bake at 350° for 1 hour. **Yield:** 6-8 servings.

TOMATO TIPS: Immature green tomatoes never ripen, but they can be cooked or pickled.
● Tomatoes can be frozen if you plan to stew them or use them in cooking.
● Add tomatoes to the salad just before serving to keep the juice from diluting the dressing.
● Tomatoes with the stems attached lose moisture more slowly and stay fresh longer.

SPOON BREAD
Lillie Lowery, Kennesaw, Georgia

(PICTURED ON PAGE 20)

1 pint sweet milk
6 tablespoons butter
1 cup cornmeal
1 teaspoon salt
3 eggs, separated (room temperature)

Scald milk (do not boil); stir in butter, cornmeal and salt. Cook, stirring constantly, until cornmeal comes away from sides of pan and thickens. Set aside to cool to lukewarm. Add beaten egg yolks; mix thoroughly. Fold in stiffly beaten egg whites; mix gently but thoroughly. Pour into greased and floured 2-qt. baking dish and bake at 375° for 1 hour or until top is golden brown. Serve immediately. **Yield:** 6 servings.

SPICY ENGLISH MUFFINS
Kathie Mathae, Arlington, Virginia

6 English muffins
12 teaspoons butter
1 pound bulk hot pork sausage
1 jar (5 ounces) Old English cheese spread

Split English muffins; toast and butter each half. Brown sausage; pour off grease. Mix sausage and cheese spread thoroughly. Spread 1/12 of mixture on each muffin half; press down firmly. Heat in toaster oven or microwave, or freeze and keep for quick breakfast. **Yield:** 12 muffin halves.

HEARTY HUEVOS RANCHEROS
Jann Voelz, Roberts, Montana

1 flour tortilla, heated
1/3 cup mild chili con carne, heated thoroughly
1 medium egg, cooked over-easy
1/4 cup finely shredded cheddar cheese
1 tablespoon mild green chilies, chopped

Place warmed tortilla on breakfast plate. Spoon chili on tortilla; spread only to size of cooked egg. Place egg on chili; sprinkle with the cheese and chilies. **Yield:** 1 serving.

STUFFED VIDALIA ONIONS
Suzanne McKinley, Lyons, Georgia

(PICTURED ON PAGE 21)

4 large Vidalia onions, peeled*
1 package (10 ounces) frozen green peas
4 ounces fresh mushrooms, sliced
1/4 teaspoon thyme leaves, crushed
1/8 teaspoon pepper
2 tablespoons butter *or* margarine
1/4 cup hot water
1/2 teaspoon instant chicken bouillon granules

(*Substitute any large, sweet onions if Vidalias are not available.) Slice tops off onions; hollow out center of each onion, leaving 1/4-in.-thick shell. Place onion shells in 8-in. x 8-in. baking dish. Combine peas, mushrooms, thyme and pepper. Fill each onion with one-fourth of vegetable mixture. Dot each with 1/2 tablespoon butter; set aside. Combine water and bouillon; pour over onions. Cover dish with plastic wrap, turning back one edge to vent steam. Microwave on HIGH 7-10 minutes, or until tender, rotating onions halfway through cooking time. Baste with cooking liquid. Let stand, covered, 3 minutes before serving. **Yield:** 4 servings.

GRANDMOTHER'S CHICKEN 'N' DUMPLINGS
Cynthia Carroll, Cary, North Carolina

(PICTURED ON PAGE 21)

1 large chicken (6 pounds)
2 teaspoons salt
4 quarts water
2 tablespoons vinegar
1 large onion, sliced
2 carrots, washed and chopped
2 stalks celery, washed and sliced
DUMPLINGS:
2 cups all-purpose flour
1-1/2 teaspoons salt
1 egg
1/2 cup reserved chicken broth

Place chicken, salt, water, vinegar, onion, carrots and celery in large soup kettle, adding more water, if necessary, to cover chicken. Bring to boil. Cover; reduce heat to simmer. Cook until meat nearly falls from the bone. Strain off broth, reserving chicken meat. Remove and discard skin, bones and vegetables. Cut or tear meat into bite-size pieces. Reserve 1 cup broth; cool to lukewarm. To make dumplings, combine flour and salt. Make a "well" in flour; add egg. Gradually stir 1/4 cup broth into egg, picking up flour as you go. Continue until flour is used up, adding additional broth as needed, and dough is consistency of pie dough. Pour any remaining reserved broth back into soup kettle. Turn the dough onto a floured surface; knead in additional flour to make stiff dough. Allow dough to rest 15 minutes. Roll out dough on floured surface as if for pie crust (circle about 17 in. round). Cut into pieces 1 in. square. Dust with additional flour; lay aside to dry for 30 to 60 minutes. Bring chicken broth to boil (you should have about 4 qts). Drop squares into boiling broth; reduce heat to slow simmer. Cover; simmer for 10 minutes. Uncover; cook until a dough dumpling tests done, about 30 minutes. Dust with pepper and add reserved chicken meat. **Yield:** 8-10 servings.

BLACK BEAN SOUP
Mickey and Don Ertel, Barefoot Bay, Florida

(PICTURED ON PAGE 21)

1 pound black beans (Frijoles Negros)
1-1/2 pounds slab bacon *or* 2 smoked ham hocks (1-1/2 to 2 pounds)
8 cups water
2 teaspoons celery salt
About 2 cups chicken *or* beef broth
1-1/2 tablespoons olive oil
1-1/2 cups finely chopped, seeded, cored green peppers
1-1/2 cups finely chopped onions
1-1/2 tablespoons finely minced garlic
1 teaspoon ground cumin
1 can (19 ounces) tomatoes, peeled, diced, with juice, about 2-1/2 cups
1/4 cup red wine vinegar
2 tablespoons finely chopped fresh coriander, optional
Hard-cooked egg, sieved

Place beans, bacon/ham hocks, water and celery salt in heavy kettle. Bring to boil; cover and simmer about 2-1/2 hours or until beans are thoroughly tender. Remove bacon/ham hocks; set aside. Drain beans and reserve along with meat and cooking liquid. (There should be about 6 cups of beans and 4 cups of liquid.) Add enough broth to make 6 cups liquid. Combine the beans with liquid in large bowl. Heat oil in heavy kettle; add peppers, onions, garlic and cumin. Cook, stirring, until onions are wilted. Add tomatoes and vinegar. Let simmer about 15 minutes. Meanwhile, remove and discard skin from bacon, or skin and bones from ham hocks. Chop ham; set aside. Add bean mixture to cooked tomato mixture. Add chopped meat and coriander. Simmer until thoroughly heated. Serve in soup bowls; garnish with sieved hard-cooked egg, if desired. **Yield:** 8-10 servings.

PRALINE/ YAM CASSEROLE
Alice Mathews, Alexandria, Louisiana

(PICTURED ON PAGE 21)

4 medium yams
2 eggs
1/2 cup brown sugar, *divided*
2 tablespoons butter, melted
1/2 teaspoon salt
1/2 cup pecan halves
1/4 cup melted butter
ORANGE SAUCE:
1/3 cup sugar
1 tablespoon cornstarch
1/8 teaspoon salt
1 teaspoon grated orange peel
1 cup orange juice
1 tablespoon lemon juice
2 tablespoons butter

Cook yams in microwave or on top of stove until tender. Peel and mash in large bowl. Beat in eggs, 1/4 cup of brown sugar, butter and salt. Spoon mixture into 1-qt. buttered casserole. Arrange pecan halves over top. Sprinkle with remaining 1/4 cup brown sugar; drizzle with 1/4 cup melted butter. Bake, uncovered, at 375° for 20 minutes. To make sauce, combine sugar, cornstarch, salt, orange peel, orange and lemon juice in saucepan. Bring to boil over medium heat, stirring until sauce is thickened. Remove from heat; stir in butter. Serve warm orange sauce over casserole. **Yield:** 6 servings.

BLACKBERRY COBBLER

Trudy Cinque, Waynesville, North Carolina

(PICTURED ON PAGE 22)

1/2 cup butter *or* margarine

SYRUP:
1 cup sugar
1 cup water

COBBLER:
1-1/2 cups of *self-rising* flour*
1/2 cup butter *or* margarine
1/3 cup milk, room temperature
2 cups blackberries, fresh
   or frozen
1/2 to 1 teaspoon cinnamon
2 tablespoons sugar

(*If self-rising flour is not available, substitute 1-1/2 cups all-purpose flour plus 1/4 teaspoon salt and 2-1/4 teaspoons baking powder.) Melt 1/2 cup butter in 10-in. round or oval baking dish; set aside. Heat sugar and water until sugar melts; set aside. Make cobbler dough by cutting butter/margarine into flour until particles are like fine crumbs. Add milk and stir with a fork until dough leaves sides of bowl. Turn out on floured board; knead 3 or 4 times. Roll out to 11-in. x 9-in. x 1/4-in. thick rectangle. Spread berries over dough; sprinkle with cinnamon and roll up like jelly roll. Cut into 1-1/4-in.-thick slices. Carefully place in pan over melted butter. Pour sugar syrup carefully around slices (crust will absorb liquid). Bake at 350° for 1 hour. (Fifteen minutes before removing from oven, sprinkle 2 tablespoons sugar over crust.) Serve warm or cold. **Yield:** 8 servings.

BANANA SPICE CAKE

Meredith Barrett, Dalton, Georgia

(PICTURED ON PAGE 22)

CAKE:
2-1/2 cups sifted cake flour
1-2/3 cups sugar
1-1/4 teaspoons baking powder
1-1/4 teaspoons baking soda
1 teaspoon salt
1-1/2 teaspoons cinnamon
3/4 teaspoon nutmeg
1/2 teaspoon ground cloves
2/3 cup solid vegetable
   shortening
2/3 cup buttermilk
1-1/4 cups mashed ripe bananas
   (3 medium)
2 eggs, unbeaten

SEA FOAM FROSTING:
2 egg whites
1-1/2 cups brown sugar
5 tablespoons water
Dash salt
1 teaspoon vanilla
1 banana, sliced

CHOCOLATE GARNISH:
2 squares sweet baking
   chocolate
1 tablespoon butter

To make cake, sift together flour, sugar, baking powder, soda, salt, cinnamon, nutmeg and cloves. Add shortening, buttermilk and mashed bananas; mix until flour is dampened. Beat at low speed for 2 minutes. Add eggs; beat 1 minute. Bake in two 9-in. greased and floured layer pans at 350° for about 40 minutes or until cake tests done. Remove from pans; cool on wire racks. To make frosting, combine egg whites, sugar, water and salt in top of 6-cup double boiler; beat slightly to mix. Place over rapidly boiling water; beat with mixer at high speed until frosting stands in peaks, about 7 minutes. Remove from heat. Add vanilla; beat 1 to 2 minutes or until thick enough to spread. Spread frosting between cooled layers; top with banana slices; put layers together. Frost cake, drizzling melted chocolate/butter mixture in pattern of choice over frosting. **Yield:** 12-14 servings.

BANANA PUDDING

Doris Clayton, Germantown, Tennessee

(PICTURED ON PAGE 22)

3 packages (3-1/2 ounces each)
   instant vanilla pudding/pie
   filling mix
5 cups milk
1 carton (8 ounces) dairy
   sour cream
1 carton (12 ounces) frozen
   nondairy topping, thawed
   and divided *or* 8 ounces
   whipping cream, whipped to
   stiff peaks
2 boxes (8 ounces each)
   vanilla wafers
12 to 15 bananas, sliced

In large mixing bowl, blend pudding mix in milk with wire whisk. Add sour cream and *one-half* whipped topping, mixing well. Set aside. In large, deep glass bowl, alternate cookies, bananas and pudding mixture in layers. Top with reserved whipped topping and additional banana slices, if desired. Refrigerate overnight. **Yield:** 16 servings.

TEXAS PECAN PIE

Helen Suter, Rosenberg, Texas

(PICTURED ON PAGE 22)

5 eggs
3 tablespoons butter, soft
   or melted
1/2 cup white sugar
1-1/4 cups white corn syrup
1 teaspoon vanilla
1/4 teaspoon salt
3 tablespoons flour
2 cups pecan halves
1 unbaked 9- *or* 10-inch pie
   shell*

Beat eggs lightly. Add butter, sugar, syrup, vanilla, salt, flour and pecans. Pour into pie shell (*9-in. pie will be full). Bake at 350° for about 40 minutes or until center is soft but not quite set.

SPICY COCHILLA CHOWDER

Gloria Piantek, Skillman, New Jersey

1 can (1 pound, 12 ounces)
   pork and beans
2 jars (12 ounces *each*) medium
   hot chunky salsa
1 pound cooked smoked
   sausage, cut in 1/2-inch
   rounds
2 cups nacho cheese-flavored
   corn chips, broken
1 cup shredded cheddar
   cheese

Combine pork and beans, salsa and sausage in 2-1/2 quart casserole dish. Cover; cook 6 minutes on HIGH in microwave; stir and continue cooking for 6 more minutes until mixture is hot. Sprinkle with chips, then cheese and MW on HIGH for 2 minutes or until cheese is melted. **Yield:** 6-8 servings.

VEGGIE HOW-TOS: To keep cauliflower white while cooking, add a little milk to the water.

● When boiling corn, add sugar to the water instead of salt. Salt toughens the corn.

● To ripen tomatoes, put them in a paper bag in a dark pantry, and they will ripen overnight.

● Do not use soda to keep vegetables green—it destroys vitamin C.

● When cooking cabbage, place a small cup or can half full of vinegar on the stove near the cabbage. It will absorb all the cabbage odor.

OVEN FRENCH TOAST WITH NUT TOPPING
Donna Justin, Sparta, Wisconsin

(PICTURED ON PAGE 24)

1 loaf (12 ounces) French bread, cut in 1-inch slices
8 large eggs
2 cups milk
2 cups half-and-half
2 teaspoons vanilla
1/2 teaspoon nutmeg
1/2 teaspoon cinnamon
1/2 teaspoon mace
TOPPING:
3/4 cup butter, softened
1-1/3 cups brown sugar
3 tablespoons dark corn syrup
1-1/3 cups coarsely chopped pecans *or* walnuts *or* hickory nuts

Heavily butter 13-in. x 9-in. x 2-in. baking pan. Fill pan with bread slices to within 1/2 in. of top. Set aside. In blender, mix eggs, milk, half-and-half, vanilla, nutmeg, cinnamon and mace. Pour mixture over bread slices. Refrigerate, covered, overnight. Make topping by combining all ingredients; set aside until time to bake toast. Spread topping over toast; bake at 350° for 50 minutes until puffed and golden. (Shield top with foil if top browns too quickly.) **Yield:** 8-10 servings.

COFFEE CAKE WHEELS
Sue Pipkin, Baxter Springs, Kansas

(PICTURED ON PAGE 24)

1 cup butter
1/2 cup sugar
1/2 teaspoon salt
2 tablespoons grated lemon rind
2 eggs, well beaten
1 package active dry yeast
1/4 cup warm water (110°-115°)
1 cup dairy sour cream
4-1/2 cups sifted flour
1/4 cup melted butter, *divided*
1/4 cup brown sugar
6 tablespoons sugar
1-1/2 teaspoons cinnamon
3/4 cup chopped nuts
3/4 cup raisins

Cream together butter and sugar until fluffy. Add salt, lemon rind, eggs and yeast which has been dissolved in warm water. Blend in sour cream. Add flour; mix thoroughly. Chill, covered, in refrigerator for 3 hours. Remove from refrigerator; let rise for 1-1/2 hours. Cover bottom of 13-in. x 9-in. x 2-in. baking pan with 3 tablespoons melted butter; sprinkle on brown sugar. Roll dough on lightly floured board into 22-in. x 16-in. x 1/4-in.-thick rectangle. Brush dough with remaining butter. Combine sugar and cinnamon; sprinkle evenly over dough. Sprinkle nuts and raisins evenly over dough. Roll up long edge like jelly roll; seal edges. Cut crosswise into 3/4-in.-thick slices. Arrange slices on top of brown sugar-butter mixture in pan. Cover; let rise in warm place until double. (Can refrigerate and bake next day—allow up to 1-1/2 hours rising time before baking.) Bake at 375° for 35 minutes. **Yield:** 16 servings.

HOT FRUIT COMPOTE
Jean Saveraid, Huxley, Iowa

(PICTURED ON PAGE 24)

1 can (20 ounces) pineapple chunks
1 can (16 ounces) peach halves
1 can (16 ounces) pear halves
1 can (16 ounces) apricot halves
1 jar maraschino cherries
ORANGE SAUCE:
1/3 cup sugar
2 tablespoons cornstarch
1/4 teaspoon salt
1/2 cup light corn syrup
1 cup orange juice
2 tablespoons orange rind

Drain fruit; arrange in a 13-in. x 9-in. x 2-in. baking dish with cherries in hollows. Set aside. To make sauce, combine sugar, cornstarch, salt, corn syrup, orange juice and rind in pan; heat to a boil. Remove; pour sauce over fruit compote. Bake at 350° for 30 minutes. **Yield:** 12 servings.

CHANGE OF PACE: Instead of your usual bacon and eggs, try some homemade granola served with canned peaches …"fruit soup" sprinkled with granola and topped with yogurt…zucchini and oat bran muffins…or homemade pancakes served with hot spiced apple sauce.

BREAKFAST PIZZA
Wilma Richey, Lead Hill, Arkansas

(PICTURED ON PAGE 24)

1 pound bulk pork sausage, crumbled
1 package (8 ounces) refrigerated crescent rolls
1 cup frozen loose-pack hash brown potatoes, thawed
1 cup (4 ounces) shredded sharp cheddar cheese
5 eggs
1/4 cup milk
1/2 teaspoon salt
1/4 teaspoon pepper
2 tablespoons grated Parmesan cheese

In skillet, cook sausage until browned. Drain; set aside. Separate dough into eight triangles. Arrange on ungreased 12-in. pizza pan with points toward center. Press over bottom and up sides to form crust, *sealing perforations completely*. Spoon sausage over crust. Sprinkle with potatoes. Top with cheddar cheese; set aside. Beat together eggs, milk, salt and pepper in mixing bowl; pour over filling. Sprinkle Parmesan cheese over all. Bake at 375° for 25-30 minutes. **Yield:** 6-8 servings.

DUTCH HONEY SYRUP
Mary Grob, Tucson, Arizona

1 cup dark corn syrup
1 cup granulated sugar
1 teaspoon salt
2 tablespoons butter
1/2 cup evaporated milk
1/2 teaspoon coconut extract

Combine syrup, sugar, salt, butter and milk. Cook over medium heat, stirring constantly, until mixture *begins* to boil—do not allow to boil. Gently simmer 3 minutes, stirring occasionally. Remove from heat; add coconut extract.

OATMEAL WAFFLES
Marna Heitz, Farley, Iowa

(PICTURED ON PAGE 25)

 This tasty dish uses less sugar, salt and fat. Recipe includes *Diabetic Exchanges.*

1-1/2 cups all-purpose flour
   1 cup quick-cooking rolled oats
   1 tablespoon baking powder
  1/2 teaspoon cinnamon
  1/4 teaspoon salt, optional
   2 eggs, slightly beaten
1-1/2 cups milk
   6 tablespoons butter, melted
   2 tablespoons brown sugar

In large mixing bowl, stir together flour, oats, baking powder, cinnamon and salt; set aside. In small mixing bowl, stir together eggs, milk, butter and brown sugar. Add to flour mixture; stir until blended. Pour batter onto grids of preheated, lightly greased waffle iron (amount will vary with size of waffle iron). Close lid quickly; *do not open during baking.* Use fork to remove baked waffle. Top with fresh fruit and yogurt. **Yield:** 12 waffles (4 inches square each), about 6 servings. **Diabetic Exchanges:** One serving equals 1 bread, 2 fats; also, 176 calories, 223 mg sodium, 65 mg cholesterol, 21 gm carbohydrate, 5 gm protein, 8 gm fat.

SPINACH QUICHE
Lois Dethloff, Amboy, Minnesota

(PICTURED ON PAGE 25)

   1 package (10 ounces) frozen, chopped spinach
   1 package (8 ounces) refrigerated crescent rolls
1-1/4 cups shredded Swiss cheese
  1/4 cup finely minced onion
   5 eggs
  3/4 cup milk
   2 teaspoons Worcestershire sauce
  1/2 teaspoon salt
  1/8 teaspoon pepper
   8 slices bacon—fried crisp, drained and crumbled
Fresh chopped parsley
Parmesan cheese

Cook spinach according to package directions. Drain well; squeeze out excess moisture. Chop into smaller pieces; set aside. Unroll dough; press into greased 10-in. glass pie plate, covering bottom and sides. Sprinkle cheese and onion over crust. Beat eggs; add milk, seasonings and reserved spinach. Pour into crust. Sprinkle with bacon, parsley and Parmesan cheese. Bake at 350° for 40-45 minutes or until a knife inserted near center comes out clean. Let stand a minimum of 5 minutes before serving. **Yield:** 6-8 servings.

HELPFUL HINTS: For extra-light pancakes, turn as soon as pancakes puff up and fill with bubbles. If you wait until the bubbles break, pancakes will be tough.
  ● Leftover French toast freezes well. Reheat in oven, microwave or toaster.
  ● When the grocery has "very ripe" bananas on sale, buy a bunch. Peel, bag and freeze them. Then, when you make banana muffins or bread, remove as many bananas as the recipe calls for, thaw, mash and use as usual.

LEMON YOGURT MUFFINS
Bev Neuenschwander, Dalton, Ohio

(PICTURED ON PAGE 25)

 This tasty dish uses less sugar, salt and fat. Recipe includes *Diabetic Exchanges.*

   2 cups all-purpose flour
   1 teaspoon baking powder
   1 teaspoon baking soda
  1/4 teaspoon salt
  1/4 cup sugar
   2 tablespoons honey
   2 eggs
1-1/4 cups (14 ounces) plain yogurt, room temperature
  1/4 cup melted butter
   1 tablespoon grated lemon peel
LEMON SYRUP:
  1/3 cup lemon juice
  1/3 cup sugar
   3 tablespoons water

Combine flour, baking powder, soda and salt; set aside. In another bowl, combine sugar, honey, eggs, yogurt, butter and rind. Add dry ingredients; mix. Spoon into greased muffin tins. Bake at 375° for 15 minutes or until wooden pick in center tests done. To make syrup, combine ingredients in a saucepan; boil 1 minute. Drizzle syrup over warm muffins. **Yield:** 12 muffins. **Diabetic Exchanges:** One serving equals 2 breads, 1 fat; also, 188 calories, 213 mg sodium, 57 mg cholesterol, 31 gm carbohydrate, 5 gm protein, 5 gm fat.

CHILI CHEESE STRATA
Shirley Smith, Anaheim, California

(PICTURED ON PAGE 25)

   1 loaf (12 ounces) French bread, cut in 1-inch cubes
   2 cups shredded cheddar *or* Monterey Jack cheese, *divided*
   1 jar (8 ounces) mild green chili salsa *or* 4 ounces chopped green chilies and 4 ounces salsa, combined
   4 eggs
   1 can (11 ounces) condensed cheddar cheese soup
   2 cups milk *or* half-and-half
   2 tablespoons minced onion
   1 teaspoon Worcestershire sauce
Paprika

In buttered 2-qt. shallow dish, arrange bread cubes evenly. Sprinkle 1 cup cheese evenly over cubes. Pour chili salsa to cover evenly; set aside. In blender, combine eggs, soup, milk, onion, Worcestershire sauce; pour over bread mixture. Top with remaining cheese. Cover; refrigerate 6 hours or overnight. Uncover; dust top with paprika. Bake at 350° for 30 minutes or until lightly browned and bubbly. **Yield:** 8 servings.

MOM'S ONION CUSTARD
Patricia Tollis, Newark, Delaware

   1 pound white onions
  1/4 cup butter
   3 eggs
  1/4 cup heavy cream
  1/2 teaspoon nutmeg
  1/4 teaspoon salt
Pinch of pepper
   1 strip of lean bacon

Peel onions; let stand in cold salted water for 1 hour. Drain onions; slice and saute in butter in large heavy skillet. Cook onions until soft, but *do not brown.* Cool. Beat eggs; add cream, nutmeg, salt and pepper. Mix with onions. Pour into buttered 1-1/2-qt. casserole or 10-inch quiche pan. Slice bacon into tiny strips (pre-cook for 10 seconds on HIGH in microwave, if desired) and sprinkle on top of custard. Bake at 350° for 20 minutes. **Yield:** 6 servings.

BUTTERMILK CRANBERRY MUFFINS
Jane Yunker, Rochester, New York

(PICTURED ON PAGE 26)

✓ This tasty dish uses less sugar, salt and fat. Recipe includes *Diabetic Exchanges*.

- 1 heaped cup of cranberries, coarsely chopped
- 3/4 cup sugar, *divided*
- 3 cups all-purpose flour
- 3-1/2 teaspoons baking powder
- 1/4 teaspoon baking soda, optional
- 1/2 teaspoon salt
- 1/2 cup butter
- 1 egg
- 1-1/2 cups buttermilk, room temperature
- 2 tablespoons frozen orange juice concentrate, thawed

CRANBERRY BUTTER:
- 1 cup cranberries
- 1 cup confectioners' sugar
- 1/2 cup butter
- 1 tablespoon lemon juice

Chop the cranberries and combine with 1/4 cup sugar; set aside. Sift together flour, remaining sugar, baking powder, soda and salt. Cut in butter until mixture resembles coarse meal. Lightly beat together egg, buttermilk and orange juice concentrate. Add the liquid and sweetened cranberries to dry ingredients, stirring only until well-combined. Spoon batter in buttered muffin pans, filling them two-thirds full. Bake at 375° for 25 minutes. To make cranberry butter, puree cranberries in food processor or blender. Add sugar, butter and lemon juice; process until smooth. Refrigerate until ready to use. **Yield:** 18 muffins. **Diabetic Exchanges:** One serving equals 1 bread, 1 fruit, 1 fat; also, 173 calories, 209 mg sodium, 30 mg cholesterol, 27 gm carbohydrate, 3 gm protein, 6 gm fat.

SOUTHERN PLANTATION CORN BREAD
Beverly Plymell, Keytesville, Missouri

(PICTURED ON PAGE 26)

- 1 cup butter, *divided*
- 4 tablespoons flour
- 1 pint half-and-half
- 4 slices American cheese
- 1 carton (8 ounces) whipping cream
- 1 egg, beaten
- 1 carton (8 ounces) dairy sour cream
- 2 boxes (8-1/2 ounces *each*) corn muffin mix
- 6 ounces diced breakfast ham or 1-1/2 cups diced ham

Melt 1/2 cup of butter. Add flour and half-and-half; cook until slightly thickened. Crumble in cheese; blend. Cool. Add whipping cream, beaten egg and sour cream, blending each. Add remaining butter (melted); fold in corn muffin mix. Fold in ham. Spread in 13-in. x 9-in. x 2-in. baking pan. Bake at 350° for 50-60 minutes or until set. *Do not overbake—should be moist.* **Yield:** 12-15 servings.

SCRAMBLED EGG CASSEROLE
Mary Anne McWhirter, Pearland, Texas

(PICTURED ON PAGE 26)

CHEESE SAUCE:
- 2 tablespoons butter
- 2-1/2 tablespoons flour
- 2 cups milk
- 1/2 teaspoon salt
- 1/8 teaspoon ground pepper
- 1 cup American cheese, shredded
- 1 cup cubed ham
- 1/4 cup chopped green onion
- 3 tablespoons melted butter
- 1 dozen eggs, beaten
- 1 can (4 ounces) sliced mushrooms, drained

TOPPING:
- 1/4 cup melted butter
- 2-1/4 cups soft bread crumbs

To make cheese sauce, melt butter, blend in flour and cook for 1 minute. Gradually stir in milk; cook until thick. Add salt, pepper and cheese; stir until cheese melts. Set aside. Saute ham and green onion in 3 tablespoons butter until onion is tender. Add eggs and cook over medium heat until eggs are set; stir in the mushrooms and cheese sauce. Spoon eggs into greased 13-in. x 9-in. x 2-in. baking pan. Combine topping ingredients; spread evenly over egg mixture. Cover; chill overnight. Uncover; bake at 350° for 30 minutes. **Yield:** 10-12 servings.

BREAKFAST FUN: Put more cheer into the morning for kids by using a cookie cutter to cut a shape from the center of a bread slice. Dip the slice and cutout into melted butter and place side by side on preheated griddle; crack open an egg inside the hole in the bread. Fry until egg is set; carefully remove the egg and toast together and serve.

QUICHE ITALIANO
Caryn Wiggins, Columbus, Indiana

(PICTURED ON PAGE 26)

- Pastry for 1 pie shell (10 inches), unbaked
- 2-1/2 ounces (1/2 cup) pepperoni, thinly sliced and halved
- 3 tablespoons chopped green pepper
- 2 tablespoons chopped onion
- 1 jar (2-1/2 ounces) sliced mushrooms, drained
- 1 tablespoon butter
- 1/2 teaspoon crushed, dried oregano
- 1/2 teaspoon fennel seed
- 1 cup (4 ounces) shredded mozzarella cheese
- 3 eggs
- 1-1/2 cups half-and-half
- 1/2 teaspoon salt
- 1/8 teaspoon pepper
- 1 tomato, cut in wedges
- 1/4 cup (1 ounce) shredded mozzarella cheese

Line pie plate with pastry. Trim edges and flute. *Do not prick shell.* Weight shell with dried beans or metal pie weights to prevent bubbles. Bake at 400° for 5-7 minutes. Remove from oven. Remove weights; set aside. In a small skillet, cook pepperoni, green pepper, onion and mushrooms in butter until tender. Stir in oregano and fennel seeds. In pastry shell, layer 1 cup mozzarella cheese; top with pepperoni mixture. In medium bowl, combine eggs, half-and-half, salt and pepper. Beat with fork or whisk until mixed well but not frothy. Pour over pepperoni mixture in pastry. Bake at 375° for 25-30 minutes or until knife inserted off center comes out clean. Top with tomato wedges. Sprinkle quiche with remaining 1/4 cup mozzarella cheese. Bake 2 minutes longer or until cheese melts. Let stand 5 minutes before serving. **Yield:** 4-6 servings.

OVEN-BAKED SAUSAGE CASSEROLE
Patricia Crawley, Sunrise, Florida

1 pound bulk *hot* sausage
1 diced red pepper
1 diced green pepper
1 medium onion, chopped
6 eggs
1/4 cup milk
1/2 teaspoon garlic salt
1/2 teaspoon white pepper
1-1/2 cups grated sharp cheddar cheese

Crumble sausage; brown and drain. Saute the vegetables; drain. Set aside. Beat the eggs, milk, garlic salt and pepper until frothy. Layer sausage, vegetables and cheese in greased 1-1/2-qt. casserole. Top with egg mixture; bake at 350° until set, about 35 minutes. **Yield:** 6 servings.

HOMEMADE PANCAKE MIX
Brenda Rick, Litchfield, Minnesota

10 cups flour
5 rounded teaspoons baking powder
1 tablespoon baking soda
1/4 cup sugar
3 teaspoons salt, optional
3 cups corn flake crumbs
2 cups old-fashioned rolled oats
3 cups whole wheat flour

Combine all ingredients; cover and store. When ready to use, mix about *1-1/2 cups dry mix* with *1 egg* and *1-1/2 cups milk*. Bake on griddle as usual. **Yield:** 18 cups dry mix.

CRUSTLESS BACON AND EGG QUICHE
Lois Hershey, Kirkwood, Pennsylvania

8 strips bacon, diced
1-1/2 cups milk
1/2 cup prepared biscuit mix
3 eggs
1/4 cup butter, melted
Dash pepper
1 cup shredded cheddar cheese

Fry or microwave bacon until crisp; crumble and set aside. In blender combine milk, biscuit mix, eggs, butter and

pepper; blend for 15 seconds. Pour into greased 9-in. pie pan. Sprinkle bacon and cheese on top of egg mixture; gently press below surface with a fork. Bake at 350° for 30 minutes or until knife inserted halfway between center and edge comes out clean. Let stand for 10 minutes before serving. **Yield:** 4-6 servings.

ORANGE DATE MUFFINS
Margery Cunningham, Portsmouth, Rhode Island

1 cup all-purpose flour
1/2 cup sugar
1/2 teaspoon baking soda
1/2 teaspoon salt, optional
1 egg
1/2 cup vegetable oil
1/2 cup orange juice, divided
1/2 cup milk
1/2 cup finely chopped dates, tossed in flour to prevent clumping
1/2 cup chopped nuts

Stir together flour, sugar, baking soda and salt; set aside. Beat egg lightly in bowl. Beat in oil, 1/4 cup orange juice and milk. Add remaining dry ingredients, mixing just until flour is moistened (batter will not be smooth). Fold in dates and nuts. Fill greased large muffin cups (or 6-oz. Pyrex custard cups) three-fourths full. Bake at 350° 25-30 minutes or until wood pick inserted in center comes out clean. Remove from pan. Brush with remaining orange juice and roll in sugar to coat lightly. **Yield:** 6 large muffins.

SPECIAL SYRUPS: Out of pancake syrup? Make your own! Mix 1-1/2 cups of brown sugar and 1 cup of water in a small saucepan; boil 1 minute. Add 1 tablespoon butter, 1/4 teaspoon vanilla extract and 1/4 teaspoon maple flavoring.

● To make an easy fruit syrup, combine 1/2 cup water, 2 tablespoons sugar and 1/2 teaspoon lemon juice; heat until sugar dissolves. Cool. Add 1/2 cup jam or fruit preserves. Add more lemon juice to taste, if desired.

● If syrup's too sweet to suit you, make a fruit topping for pancakes, waffles or French toast. Place 2 cups fresh or frozen blueberries in a small saucepan; mix together 1 tablespoon cornstarch and 1/3 cup water and pour over berries. Cook over medium heat until thick and clear. Sweeten to taste, using artificial sweetener if desired.

DESSERT DIP WITH FRESH FRUIT PLATE
Joyce Fortney, Artemus, Kentucky

1 package (8 ounces) cream cheese, *softened*
2 tablespoons frozen orange juice concentrate
1 jar (7 ounces) marshmallow creme
Fresh fruit—apple wedges, orange rings, pineapple chunks, banana chunks, kiwi slices (dip apples and bananas in orange or lemon juice to keep them from browning)

Combine cream cheese with orange juice concentrate in mixing bowl until smooth. Fold in marshmallow creme. Serve dip in center of large glass plate surrounded by assorted fruits.

AUNT CAROL'S LAYERED COFFEE CAKE
Jackie Baumann, Greencastle, Indiana

2 cups biscuit mix
1/4 cup sugar
2/3 cup milk, room temperature
2 tablespoons vegetable oil
1 egg, room temperature

FILLING:
1 package (8 ounces) cream cheese, *softened*
1/4 cup sugar
1 egg, room temperature
1/4 teaspoon vanilla
1/4 cup raisins, plumped in 1/4 cup boiling water, *drained*
2 cups apple slices, peeled and sliced 1/4-inch thick
3 tablespoons sugar
1/4 teaspoon cinnamon

Combine mix, sugar, milk, oil and egg; beat well. Pour into greased and floured 13-in. x 9-in. x 2-in. baking dish; set aside. Beat cream cheese, sugar, egg and vanilla until smooth and well-blended. Spread cream cheese mixture evenly over batter. Sprinkle raisins over cheese mixture; set apple slices into cheese mixture. Combine sugar and cinnamon; sprinkle over apples. Bake at 350° for 35-40 minutes. **Yield:** 12 servings.

COUNTRY INNS

Glacier Bay Country Inn

Box 5, Gustavus, Alaska 99826

Phone: 1-907/697-2288

Directions: From Juneau, reach Gustavus (near Glacier Bay National Park headquarters) via jet or bush plane. If traveling on Alaska Highway, fly from Haines or Skagway. The inn provides complimentary pickup from airport.

Innkeepers: Al & Annie Unrein

Schedule: Open year-round. Dining room open to public for dinner by reservation.

Accommodations and Rates: 9 rooms, 7 with private baths, $99-$129 single, $184 double (two persons), includes three meals per night's stay. Additional persons in room; adults $69; children 3-11, $54. Inquire about special inn/adventure packages.

Glacier Bay's menus showcase fresh Alaskan seafood and vegetables. Guests rave about the homemade breads, desserts and soups.

Perhaps you'd enjoy a breakfast in bed of blueberry pancakes with homemade spruce tip syrup, bacon, coffee cake, fruit juice and coffee. Or a dinner of steamed whole Dungeness crabs, served with a carrot/broccoli and green salad picked fresh from the inn's garden and followed by Five-Chocolate Torte for dessert. Another evening, you might delight in a dinner of creamy crab bisque, baked salmon steaks, potatoes, snow peas and rhubarb custard pie!

If you're not quite ready to fly in to this remote and breathtakingly beautiful spot, try a taste of Alaska at home, with some of the recipes the Unreins shared:

ALASKAN SALMON BISQUE

- 1/2 cup butter
- 1 cup onion, chopped
- 1 cup celery, chopped
- 1/2 teaspoon white pepper
- 1 teaspoon salt (optional)
- 2 cups chicken stock
- 2 tablespoons cornstarch
- 1/2 cup cold water
- 1 teaspoon ground cumin
- 2 cups milk
- 2 cups heavy cream
- 1/4 to 1/2 cup tomato paste *or* fresh pureed tomatoes
- 1 pound fresh salmon filet, skin removed, cut in chunks, *or* canned salmon, skin and bones removed

Paprika

Saute onion in butter until transparent; add celery and cook just until tender. Add salt, white pepper and chicken stock; bring to a boil. Reduce heat. Add cornstarch dissolved in cold water; cook about 2 minutes, stirring constantly. Add cumin, milk, cream and tomato paste; bring just to a simmer—do not boil. Add fresh salmon and bring back to a boil for 1-2 minutes. (If using canned salmon, turn off heat, add salmon and let stand until salmon is heated through.) Garnish with paprika. **Yield:** 8 servings.

RICE PILAF

- 1/4 cup butter *or* margarine
- 1-1/2 cups uncooked regular long grain rice
- 3 ounces vermicelli, broken into 1-inch pieces (put pasta in a zip-lock bag while breaking it)
- 1/2 cup celery
- 1/2 cup chopped onions
- 3 cups chicken stock (3 14-1/2-ounce cans of commercial stock)
- 1/2 teaspoon white pepper
- 1/2 teaspoon salt
- 2 tablespoons chopped fresh chives

Melt butter or margarine in a heavy 2- to 2-1/2-quart saucepan. Add rice, vermicelli, celery and onions, cooking over medium-high heat, stirring frequently, until vegetables are tender and rice and vermicelli are golden brown. Add chicken stock and seasonings; bring to a boil, stirring occasionally. Reduce heat to low

simmer, cover and cook for 20 minutes without lifting cover or stirring. Remove from heat; fluff lightly with a fork; cover and let steam 5 to 10 minutes before serving. **Yield:** 6 servings.

HERB DRESSING

- 1/2 cup salad oil
- 1/3 cup white wine vinegar
- 2 tablespoons homemade salad herbs, crushed
- 1 tablespoon snipped parsley
- 1 teaspoon sugar
- 1/2 teaspoon salt
- 1/2 teaspoon freshly ground black pepper

In a jar with lid, combine all ingredients and shake until ingredients are combined. Shake well before serving. **Yield:** 1 cup.

HOMEMADE SALAD HERBS: Combine 1 tablespoon each of dried thyme, basil and tarragon. Mix together thoroughly; store in an airtight container. Use on salads, in sauces and on fish dishes.

SHRIMP AND SEASHELL SALAD

- 12 ounces small seashell macaroni, cooked and cooled
- 1/2 pound small shrimp
- 1/2 cup chopped onions
- 1 cup diced celery
- 2 tomatoes, seeded and diced
- 1/2 green pepper, seeded and diced
- 2 dozen snow peas, cut in 1-inch pieces
- 2 cups mayonnaise
- 2 tablespoons chopped fennel
- 2 tablespoons chopped dill
- 1/2 teaspoon white pepper
- 1/2 teaspoon salt

Cook seashell macaroni according to package directions; drain and cool. Combine shrimp and vegetables with macaroni in a large bowl. Blend mayonnaise, herbs and seasonings together; stir into macaroni mixture. Chill well before serving. **Yield:** 12 servings.

BEST COOK

When it comes to pleasing many palates, Sylvia Teague of Eureka Springs, Arkansas, has the knack.

"Everyone raves about Sylvia's cooking," her husband Raymond wrote in his nominating letter, "including family members, friends and guests. The Entertainment Editor of the Fort Worth, Texas, newspaper described her as a 'Renaissance Woman'.

"People who eat at our home often tell Sylvia she should start a restaurant in town. But she'd rather cook just for pleasure in her own kitchen.

"And what a pleasure it is to taste her treats! Sylvia turns our blackberries, raspberries, persimmons, wild grapes and strawberries into delicious pies, cakes, cobblers, jams and jellies. She grows her own basil for pesto, and lots of tomatoes for sauces.

"She doesn't need fancy, expensive ingredients...Sylvia makes the most of what's on hand. She bakes her own rolls, and serves an English-style breakfast every Sunday with scones or Irish soda bread."

Sylvia has loved to cook ever since she baked a batch of cookies at age 6.

"My mother was sick, and I decided to make cookies to cheer her up," she recalls. "I had to disturb her to find out the difference between 't.' and 'T.' in the recipe and what 1/2 and 1/3 were.

"I don't remember how the cookies turned out, but I know I learned the basics of reading recipes from the experience. Mom was always great about letting me make my own mistakes and discoveries.

"Nowadays I know my efforts will be rewarded by the pleasure of the people for whom I cook. The more love I put in my cooking, the more I get back!"

ALEXANDRA'S ORANGE COCONUT CAKE

2-1/4 cups whole wheat *pastry* flour*
1 tablespoon baking powder
1 teaspoon salt
5 egg yolks
1/2 cup honey
1/2 cup vegetable oil
1/2 cup orange juice
1 tablespoon grated orange rind
1/2 teaspoon cream of tartar
1 cup egg whites
1/4 cup honey
1 cup flaked coconut
FILLING:
1 pint Haagen-Dazs vanilla ice cream with orange sorbet
FROSTING:
1 pint whipping cream
2 tablespoons honey
1 teaspoon vanilla
1/2 cup shredded coconut
Fresh orange slices-garnish

*Whole wheat pastry flour is available at co-ops and health food stores. Combine flour, baking powder and salt. Add egg yolks, honey, oil, orange juice and orange rind. Beat well; set aside. Beat egg whites with cream of tartar until soft peaks form. Gradually add 1/4 cup honey; beat until mixture will stand in stiff peaks. Fold coconut into egg whites. Stir small amount of egg white mixture into flour mixture; then gently fold remaining egg whites into flour mixture. Divide among three 8-inch layer cake pans which have been lined with parchment or wax paper. *Do not grease sides of pans.* Bake at 350° for 20-25 minutes or until cake tests done with wooden pick inserted in center. Cool in pans on rack for 10 minutes. Remove from pans; cool thoroughly. Soften ice cream/sorbet. Spread between cool cake layers. Place cake in freezer. Whip cream with honey and vanilla until it holds its shape. Spread on top and sides of cake. Sprinkle liberally with coconut. Decorate with orange slices cut in one-half. Keep in freezer until ready to serve. **Yield:** 16-20 servings.

PIZZALADA

CRUST:
1 cup masa harina
1/2 teaspoon salt
About 2/3 cup boiling water

SAUCE:
1 cup water
1-1/2 tablespoons chili powder or more to taste
3 ounces tomato paste
1/2 teaspoon salt

TOPPING:
1 cup cooked pinto beans, rinsed and drained
2 cups grated Monterey Jack cheese
Sliced black olives
Chopped green onions
Sliced chilies or other peppers of choice

Mix together crust ingredients to make a stiff dough, adding more water as necessary. Knead several times; roll out to fit a 12-in. greased pizza pan. Bake at 350° for 10 minutes. (Substitute prepared corn tortillas, if desired.) To prepare the sauce, combine sauce ingredients in small saucepan; bring to boil. Spread sauce evenly over baked crust. Cover with topping ingredients and bake for 10-15 minutes more.

REFRIGERATOR ROLLS

5 cups all-purpose flour
4 teaspoons baking powder
1/2 teaspoon baking soda
2 teaspoons salt
2 packages active dry yeast
1 cup warm water (110-115°)
1/4 cup honey
2 cups buttermilk
1/2 cup vegetable oil

Mix flour, baking powder, soda and salt together. Dissolve yeast in water. Add yeast mixture, buttermilk and honey to dry ingredients. Beat well. Add oil; mix thoroughly. Cover; set in refrigerator for at least *12* hours. Spoon into well-greased muffin cups, about 3/4 full. Let stand at room temperature for about 20 minutes before baking. Bake at 400° for about 20 minutes or until light brown. (Batter will keep, covered, in refrigerator for 2-3 days.) **Yield:** 2-1/2 dozen.

If you thought the only way to serve broccoli was steamed or boiled, perhaps with a little cheese sauce, are you in for a pleasant surprise! Check out the bounty of broccoli on these pages and you'll find plenty of delicious ways to serve this vitamin-filled vegetable.

BROCCOLI BONANZA. Clockwise from lower left—**Broccoli Casserole Elegant,** Dena Fischer, Manchester, Iowa (Pg. 43); **Broccoli Corn Bread,** Carolynn Girtman, Bartow, Florida (Pg. 43); **Chinese Broccoli and Beef Salad,** Karen Armstrong, Battle Ground, Washington (Pg. 43); **Broccoli Almondine,** Connie Orsua, San Jose, California (Pg. 44); **French Chicken/ Broccoli Casserole,** Gigi Adam, Santa Maria, California (Pg. 44); **Stir-Fried Broccoli with Mushrooms and Cashews,** Judi Weidmark, Uxbridge, Ontario (Pg. 44); **Mediterranean Chicken 'n' Broccoli Salad,** Loralee Hanes, Troy, Ontario (Pg. 44); **Broccoli/Mushroom Chowder,** Lorrie Arthur, Columbus, Ohio (Pg. 43).

Here's broccoli at its best! Try some of these intriguing, change-of-pace ways to prepare this vitamin-packed vegetable—you won't see noses turned up at these delicious dishes.

Crunchy florets blend with juicy orange sections in the Fresh Broccoli/Mandarin Salad. Broccoli joins forces with spicy pork in Szechuan Pork and Broccoli—a stir-fry with a difference.

Bits of broccoli color creamy Golden Cheese/Broccoli Chowder. And broccoli mingles with other vegetables and tangy cheese for a delightfully different pasta topping in Broccoli Primavera with Cheese Sauce. Broccoli a family favorite? You bet!

BRING ON THE BROCCOLI! Top to bottom—**Fresh Broccoli/Mandarin Salad,** Connie Blommers, Pella, Iowa (Pg. 45); **Szechuan Pork and Broccoli,** Marian Stalknecht, Lawrenceville, Georgia (Pg. 45); **Broccoli Primavera with Cheese Sauce,** Sherry Krenz, Woodworth, North Dakota (Pg. 44); **Golden Cheese/Broccoli Chowder,** Nancy Schmidt, Delhi, California (Pg. 45).

MEALS IN MINUTES

FUSS-FREE FOOD that lets you feed a family in 30 minutes or less...it's every busy cook's dream!

Here's a speedy, stylish meal your family's sure to enjoy. Start by washing and slicing the new potatoes and popping them into the oven. While they bake, prepare and season the tenderloin slices and assemble the sauce ingredients.

For a vegetable, select whatever favorite's in season—such as tender asparagus...new peas...or green beans—and steam or microwave it in a couple of minutes. Dessert is a delicious combination of berries, sherbet and a topping of warmed marmalade...a colorful finish to a fine-looking—and fast—feast.

NEW POTATOES WITH DILL

- **1 pound new potatoes, unpeeled**
- **2 tablespoons butter**
- **1 teaspoon fresh dill** *or* **1/2 teaspoon dried dill**
- **1/2 teaspoon seasoned salt**

Wash potatoes; cut into 3/8-in.-thick slices. In a 12-in. x 7-1/2-in. x 2-in. baking dish, arrange potatoes in thin layer. Dot with butter, sprinkle with dill and salt. Cover and bake at 425° for 25 minutes or until tender, stirring after 15 minutes. **Yield:** 4 servings.

TENDERLOIN DIANE

- **1 pound beef tenderloin, cut into 8 slices**
- **Salt**
- **Freshly ground black pepper**
- **1 teaspoon dry mustard**
- **2 tablespoons butter**
- **2 tablespoons sliced green onion**
- **1 tablespoon lemon juice**
- **2 teaspoons Worcestershire sauce**

Sprinkle one side of tenderloin slices with salt, pepper and *half* of the dry mustard. Pound the seasonings into the meat. Repeat on the other side. In a large skillet, melt butter on medium-high heat; add meat slices in a single layer. Cook for 2 minutes on each side for medium-rare doneness. Remove to a heated serving platter. To pan juices in skillet, add the green onion, lemon juice and Worcestershire sauce. Cook and stir for 1 minute. Spoon sauce over meat. **Yield:** 4 servings.

BLUEBERRY/ ORANGE CUPS

- **1/3 cup orange marmalade**
- **1 pint orange sherbet**
- **1 cup fresh blueberries**

Heat marmalade over low heat until melted. Scoop sherbet into 4 dessert dishes; top with blueberries. Spoon warm marmalade over all. **Yield:** 4 servings.

BROCCOLI AT ITS BEST: Cut an "X" in the base of the stalk to help broccoli cook faster.

- Don't overcook broccoli—it's done when it's bright green and the stalk can be easily pierced with a fork.
- For least strong flavor and brightest color, cook fresh broccoli in a vegetable steamer.

PRESERVING BROCCOLI: To freeze broccoli, clean, wash and cut broccoli heads into desired sizes. Blanch in boiling water for 3 minutes; plunge immediately into ice water and leave until chilled. Drain well on paper towels; position in single layer on cookie sheets and freeze until firm. Transfer to freezer bags or containers. For brightest green broccoli, blanch it in the microwave!

Celebrate the special occasions of summer with a beautiful backyard buffet—country style! These recipes from readers will add a delicious difference to weddings, bridal or baby showers and graduation parties.

Sweeten the moment with glorious seasonal desserts such as fresh raspberry cake or pie, light-as-a-cloud cherry roll or irresistible strawberry and kiwi tarts.

Please everyone with pretty, portable treats—luscious lemon squares, butter-rich butterfly pastries or creamy handmade mints.

For a fine finale, serve a sparkling fruit-based punch decorated with fresh herbs and seasonal fruits. It tastes as refreshing as it looks!

SWEET STARS: Clockwise on our dessert table from lower left—**Cherries 'n' Cream Roll,** Mrs. John Nolt, Lititz, Pennsylvania (Pg. 47); **Raspberry Glace Pie/Tart,** Elizabeth Karr, Tacoma, Washington, (Pg. 46); **Fresh Raspberry Cake,** Margery Peterson, Nyssa, Oregon (Pg. 46); **Mom's Cream Cheese Mints,** Alice Sunseri, St. Louis Park, Minnesota (Pg. 47); **Strawberry/Kiwi Tarts,** Becky Duncan, Leming, Texas (Pg. 47); **Wedding Punch,** Marybeth Curran, Waukesha, Wisconsin (Pg. 48); **Butterflies,** Marianne Robinson, Valencia, Pennsylvania (Pg. 47); **Delicate Lemon Squares,** Ruby Nelson, Mountain Home, Arkansas (Pg. 47).

Main dish salads just make sense for special-occasion buffets—and for cool summer suppers, as well.

These fix-ahead salads range from spicy pepperoni flavors to zesty artichoke/rice combinations, from chicken and spinach to creamy bean/cheese/ham blends. All are pretty as a picture...and pretty easy to prepare, too. Try one today!

SAVORY SALADS: Clockwise from the lower left—**Pasta Picnic Salad**, Shirley Ramsey, Wymore, Nebraska; **Artichoke Rice Salad**, Virginia Shaw, Modesto, California; **Spinach Chicken Salad**, Kim Roe, Ventura, California; **Idaho Chef's Salad**, Gladys DeBoer, Castleford, Idaho. (All recipes can be found on page 48.)

BROCCOLI CORN BREAD
Carolynn Girtman, Bartow, Florida

(PICTURED ON PAGE 36)

1/2 cup butter, melted
1/3 cup chopped onion
1 teaspoon salt
3/4 cup cottage cheese
1 package (10 ounces) frozen chopped broccoli, thawed and drained
4 eggs, slightly beaten
1 package (8-1/2 ounces) quick corn muffin mix

In mixing bowl combine melted butter, onion, salt, cheese, broccoli and beaten eggs; blend. Stir in muffin mix. Pour into greased 13-in. x 9-in. x 2-in. baking pan. Bake at 400° for 20-25 minutes. Cut into serving-size squares. **Yield:** 12 servings.

BROCCOLI CASSEROLE ELEGANT
Dena Fischer, Manchester, Iowa

(PICTURED ON PAGE 36)

1 package (6 ounces) stuffing mix
1-1/2 cups hot water
1/4 cup butter
2 packages (10 ounces *each*) frozen broccoli spears *or* 1-1/2 pounds fresh broccoli spears*
2 tablespoons water
2 tablespoons butter
2 tablespoons flour
1 teaspoon chicken-flavored bouillon granules
3/4 cup milk
1 package (3 ounces) cream cheese, softened
1/4 teaspoon salt, if desired
1 cup (4 ounces) shredded cheddar cheese

Place hot water and butter in medium bowl; microwave (MW) on HIGH until butter melts. Add seasoning packet from stuffing mix; stir. MW on HIGH for 5 minutes. Add stuffing crumbs; stir to moisten. Cover; set aside. Place frozen broccoli in large bowl; add 2 tablespoons water. Cover; MW on HIGH for 6-8 minutes. Stir; MW on HIGH 2 minutes or until tender/crisp. Let stand, covered, for 2 minutes more. *If using fresh broccoli, place in bowl. Add water; MW on high 3-5 minutes. Spoon stuffing mixture around outside of light-

ly greased 2-qt. rectangular baking dish, leaving a well in center. Place cooked broccoli in well; set aside. Using medium bowl, MW butter for 30 seconds on MEDIUM until melted. Add flour and bouillon granules; stir in milk until smooth. MW on HIGH for 1-1/2 minutes. Stir; repeat for 30 seconds until smooth and thickened. Blend in softened cream cheese and salt. Spoon sauce over broccoli; sprinkle with cheddar cheese. MW until cheese melts, about 4 minutes. **Conventional Method:** Melt butter and add water to saucepan; add seasoning packet and cook for 5 minutes. Add crumbs; cover and set aside. Cook broccoli in 2 tablespoons water until tender/crisp. Proceed with recipe, making sauce on top of stove as for white sauce, adding cheese and salt. Spoon sauce over broccoli; sprinkle with cheese. Place under oven broiler until cheese melts. **Yield:** 10 servings.

CHINESE BROCCOLI AND BEEF SALAD
Karen Armstrong, Battle Ground, Washington

(PICTURED ON PAGE 36)

3 to 4 pounds fresh broccoli
1/2 to 3/4 cup peanut oil *or* vegetable oil
2 sweet red peppers, cut in narrow strips
4 cups sliced fresh mushrooms
1/2 cup white vinegar
1/4 cup soy sauce
1-2 teaspoons salt
2-1/2 dried hot red peppers, crushed *or* 1 teaspoon red pepper flakes
2 pounds rare roast beef, julienne cuts
1 can (8 ounces) water chestnuts, drained and sliced
1 can (8 ounces) bamboo shoots, drained

Wash broccoli. Cut off florets; reserve tender parts of stalks. Cut stalks into 3/8-in.-thick slices. In wok or large skillet, heat oil. Add broccoli stalk pieces; stir-fry for about 1 minute. Add broccoli florets; stir-fry for 3 minutes or until tender/crisp. Transfer broccoli to large bowl. Stir-fry red pepper strips for 1 to 2 minutes; add to broccoli. Stir-fry mushrooms until tender/crisp; add to broccoli. Combine vinegar, soy sauce, salt and crushed hot red pepper. Pour over broccoli mixture; toss well. Add the beef, water chestnuts and bamboo shoots. Toss; cover. Chill 2-3 hours. **Yield:** 12 servings.

BROCCOLI/ MUSHROOM CHOWDER
Lorrie Arthur, Columbus, Ohio

(PICTURED ON PAGE 36)

2 pounds fresh broccoli
8 ounces fresh mushrooms
1 cup butter
1 cup flour
4 cups chicken broth
4 cups half-and-half
1 teaspoon salt, optional
1/4 teaspoon white pepper
1/4 teaspoon tarragon leaves, crushed

Clean and cut the broccoli into 1/2-in. pieces. Steam in 1/2 cup of water until tender/crisp; do not drain. Set aside. Clean and slice mushrooms. In a large pan over medium heat, melt butter; add flour to make a roux. Cook, stirring constantly, for 2-4 minutes; do not let brown. Stir in chicken broth; bring just to a boil. Turn heat to low; add broccoli, mushrooms, half-and-half and seasonings. Heat through but do not boil. **Yield:** 8 servings.

BROCCOLI/ONION DELUXE
Leigh Moore, Heffley Creek, British Columbia

1 pound fresh *or* frozen broccoli
3 medium sweet onions, quartered
SAUCE:
4 tablespoons butter, *divided*
2 tablespoons flour
1/4 teaspoon salt
Ground pepper to taste
1 cup milk
1 package (3 ounces) cream cheese
1/2 cup (2 ounces) shredded sharp cheddar cheese
1 cup soft bread crumbs

Cut broccoli into 1-in. pieces. Cook or steam until tender; drain. Cook onions until tender; drain and set aside. In small saucepan, melt *2 tablespoons butter*. Blend in flour, salt and pepper. Add milk; cook and stir until thick and bubbly. Reduce heat; blend in cream cheese. Place vegetables in a 1-1/2-qt. casserole. Pour sauce over; mix lightly. Top with the cheddar cheese. Melt remaining butter; toss with crumbs. Cover casserole. Bake at 350° for 30 minutes. **Yield:** 4 servings.

FRENCH CHICKEN/ BROCCOLI CASSEROLE
Gigi Adam, Santa Maria, California

(PICTURED ON PAGE 37)

1 pound fresh broccoli, sliced in spears and steamed 2 minutes *or* 3 packages (10 ounces each) frozen broccoli spears, thawed
3 to 4 cups cooked chicken, skinned, boned, torn in large pieces
SAUCE:
1/3 cup butter, melted
1/4 cup cornstarch, dissolved in 1/2 cup water
1/3 cup chicken broth *or* white wine
1/4 teaspoon salt
1/4 teaspoon pepper
2 cups milk
1 jar (2 ounces) diced pimientos
1 package (8 ounces) Old English cheese, cubed *or* 8 ounces grated sharp cheddar cheese

In greased 13-in. x 9-in. x 2-in. baking dish, layer the broccoli spears and chicken pieces alternately. Set aside. In a saucepan over medium heat, combine melted butter, dissolved cornstarch, broth, seasonings, milk and pimientos. Cook until thickened. Add cheese; stir until melted. Pour warm sauce over top of chicken and broccoli layers. Bake at 350° for about 35 minutes or until bubbly. **Yield:** 6 servings.

BROCCOLI ALMONDINE
Connie Orsua, San Jose, California

(PICTURED ON PAGE 37)

1/2 cup slivered almonds (2 ounces)
1 tablespoon butter
2 packages (10 ounces each) frozen broccoli spears *or* 1-1/2 pounds fresh broccoli, washed and cut into spears
2 packages (3 ounces each) cream cheese
1/3 cup milk
1 teaspoon grated lemon peel
1 tablespoon lemon juice
1/2 teaspoon ground ginger
1/4 teaspoon salt

In small glass bowl, combine almonds and butter. Microwave (MW) on MEDIUM/HIGH for 3 minutes. Stir; MW at

MEDIUM/HIGH 2 to 3 minutes or until almonds are light brown. Set aside. Place broccoli in 2-qt. glass casserole. Cover; MW on HIGH for 8-10 minutes (3-5 minutes for fresh). Let stand, covered. Place cream cheese in 2-cup glass measure; MW on LOW 2-4 minutes or until softened. Blend in milk, peel, juice, ginger and salt. MW on MEDIUM/HIGH for 3-4 minutes or until hot. Place broccoli spears on warm serving platter; pour sauce over top. Sprinkle with almonds. **Conventional Method:** Toast almonds and butter in small saucepan until almonds are light brown. Cook broccoli on stove until tender/crisp. Blend softened cream cheese, milk, peel, juice, ginger and salt. Cook until hot. Proceed with recipe. **Yield:** 6-8 servings.

MEDITERRANEAN CHICKEN 'N' BROCCOLI SALAD
Loralee Hanes, Troy, Ontario

(PICTURED ON PAGE 37)

✓ This tasty dish uses less sugar, salt and fat. Recipe includes *Diabetic Exchanges.*

4 tablespoons unsalted butter
8 chicken breast halves, skinned and boned
1/2 cup chicken broth *or* dry white wine
2 garlic cloves, minced
1-1/2 pounds fresh broccoli
1 medium red onion, quartered and thinly sliced
1/2 cup mayonnaise
1 tablespoon fresh lemon juice
1/2 teaspoon leaf thyme
1/4 teaspoon leaf basil
1/4 teaspoon leaf oregano
1/2 teaspoon salt
1/2 teaspoon pepper *or* to taste
Fresh tomatoes
Slivered, toasted almonds for garnish

In a large skillet, melt butter over low heat. Add chicken breasts in a single layer; pour in broth. Cook, tightly covered, 8-10 minutes or until chicken is springy to the touch. Remove chicken. Add garlic to broth; cook over low heat for 1 minute. Strain, reserving garlic and liquid; cool. Trim broccoli stems in 1/8-in.-thick slices and florets in 1-in. pieces; blanch in boiling, salted water for 1 minute. Plunge broccoli in ice water. Drain well; set aside. In small bowl, combine the mayonnaise, lemon juice, thyme, basil and oregano; blend well. Whisk in reserved garlic, cooking liquid, salt and pepper. In a large serving bowl, cut chicken into 1/2-in. pieces;

add broccoli and onion. Pour on dressing; toss well. Cover; refrigerate for at least 2 hours or overnight. For individual servings, spoon salad in center of a large tomato cut into wedges. For buffet serving, ring a platter or serving plate with sliced tomatoes; spoon salad into center. Sprinkle with toasted almonds. **Yield:** 8-10 servings. **Diabetic Exchanges:** One serving equals 2 meats, 4 vegetables, 3 fats; also, 415 calories, 277 mg sodium, 106 mg cholesterol, 18 gm carbohydrate, 19 gm protein, 24 gm fat.

STIR-FRIED BROCCOLI WITH MUSHROOMS AND CASHEWS
Judi Weidmark, Uxbridge, Ontario

(PICTURED ON PAGE 37)

✓ This tasty dish uses less sugar, salt and fat. Recipe includes *Diabetic Exchanges.*

2 tablespoons salad oil
1 pound fresh broccoli, cut in florets
1 teaspoon sugar
1/2 teaspoon salt
1/2 pound fresh mushrooms, cut in 1/4-inch slices
2 green onions, finely chopped
1/4 teaspoon ground nutmeg
Dry-roasted cashews

Heat 1 tablespoon oil in wok or large skillet. Add broccoli, sugar and salt; stir-fry for 3 minutes or until broccoli is tender/crisp. Add remaining oil, mushrooms, onions and nutmeg; stir-fry until added vegetables are tender/crisp, about 1-2 minutes. Sprinkle on cashews; serve hot. **Yield:** 6 servings. **Diabetic Exchanges:** One serving equals 2 vegetables, 1-1/2 fats; also, 125 calories, 196 mg sodium, 0 cholesterol, 10 gm carbohydrate, 5 gm protein, 9 gm fat.

BROCCOLI PRIMAVERA WITH CHEESE SAUCE
Sherry Krenz, Woodworth, North Dakota

(PICTURED ON PAGE 38)

4 tablespoons olive oil *or* vegetable oil
1 garlic clove, sliced
1 medium head of broccoli, cut into 2-inch x 1-inch pieces
1 small red pepper, diced
3/4 cup green onions, sliced
1 cup fresh sliced mushrooms *or* 1 can (4 ounces) canned mushrooms, drained

1/2 cup celery, diced
1 cup milk
5 ounces processed cheese spread, cubed
1/4 cup Parmesan cheese
1/2 teaspoon leaf oregano
1/2 pound ground beef *or* bulk Italian sausage, cooked and crumbled (optional)
Cooked spaghetti

In large skillet, heat oil. Cook garlic until browned; discard garlic. Add broccoli, red pepper, onion, mushrooms and celery; cook, stirring constantly, until tender/crisp. Add the milk, cubed cheese, Parmesan cheese and oregano, cooking and stirring until cheese melts. Add meat if desired. Serve over hot, cooked pasta. **Yield:** 8 servings.

SZECHUAN PORK AND BROCCOLI
Marian Stallknecht, Lawrenceville, Georgia

(PICTURED ON PAGE 38)

✓ This tasty dish uses less sugar, salt and fat. Recipe includes *Diabetic Exchanges*.

1 pound fresh lean pork (tenderloin *or* roast)
6 to 8 green onions
1 green *or* red sweet pepper
1-1/2 cups fresh broccoli
1 large onion
12 edible-pod peas
3 tablespoons peanut oil *or* vegetable oil
SAUCE:
2 cloves garlic, sliced
2 slices fresh ginger, chopped
1/4 teaspoon crushed red pepper flakes
2 tablespoons hot water
2 teaspoons sugar
6 tablespoons catsup*
4 tablespoons soy sauce*

Cut pork into narrow 1-in. strips, 1/4 in. thick; set aside. (Partially freeze pork first for easier cutting.) Cut green onions, peppers, broccoli and onion into 1-in. pieces; set aside. Combine garlic, ginger, pepper flakes, hot water, sugar, catsup and soy sauce (*can substitute 8 tablespoons prepared hoisin sauce for the catsup and soy sauce); set aside. In wok or large skillet, heat peanut or vegetable oil over high heat. Stir-fry the pork in oil until browned; remove from wok and keep warm. Add more oil if necessary and stir-fry all vegetables tender/crisp. Add pork and sauce mixture; cook until thickened. Serve with boiled rice. **Yield:** 8 servings. **Diabetic Exchanges:** One serving equals 1 meat, 2 vegetables, 2 fats;

also, 228 calories, 666 mg sodium, 50 mg cholesterol, 11 gm carbohydrate, 10 gm protein, 17 gm fat.

GOLDEN CHEESE/ BROCCOLI CHOWDER
Nancy Schmidt, Delhi, California

(PICTURED ON PAGE 38)

2 cups water
1 cup celery, chopped
1 cup carrots, chopped
1/2 cup onion, chopped
1 pound fresh broccoli, washed and chopped
CHEESE SAUCE:
1/2 cup butter
1/2 cup flour
2 teaspoons salt *or* to taste
1/4 teaspoon white pepper
4 cups milk
Tabasco sauce, as desired
1 pound processed cheese spread, cut in 1/2-inch cubes *or* 4 cups grated cheddar cheese
2 cups ham, cut in 1/2-inch cubes

In large saucepan, combine water, celery, carrots and onion. Bring to boil; reduce heat. Simmer, covered, for about 5 minutes or until tender/crisp. Add broccoli; cook until broccoli is tender/crisp, about 4-5 minutes. (To keep broccoli bright green, leave the cover slightly ajar.) *Do not drain vegetables.* To make sauce, melt butter in large saucepan; blend in flour, salt and pepper. Cook, stirring, for 1 minute. Stir in milk; cook until mixture thickens. Add several drops of Tabasco sauce if desired. Stir in the cheese and cook until melted; add the ham cubes. Combine cheese mixture with undrained vegetables; stir to blend. **Yield:** 12 servings.

FRESH BROCCOLI/ MANDARIN SALAD
Connie Blommers, Pella, Iowa

(PICTURED ON PAGE 38)
CUSTARD DRESSING:
1 egg plus 1 egg yolk, lightly beaten
1/2 cup sugar
1-1/2 teaspoons cornstarch
1 teaspoon dry mustard
1/4 cup vinegar
1/4 cup water
3 tablespoons butter, softened
1/2 cup mayonnaise

4 cups fresh broccoli florets, 1-inch cuts
1/2 cup golden raisins
6 slices bacon, cooked and crumbled
2 cups sliced fresh mushrooms
1/2 cup slivered almonds, toasted
1 can (11 ounces) mandarin oranges, drained
1/2 medium red onion, sliced in 1/8-inch-thick rings

In top of double boiler, whisk together egg, egg yolk, sugar, cornstarch and mustard. Combine vinegar and water; slowly whisk into egg mixture. Place over hot water and cook, stirring constantly, until mixture thickens. Remove from heat; stir in butter and mayonnaise. Chill. Toss dressing with remaining ingredients in serving bowl. Serve, store chilled. **Yield:** 10-12 servings.

SALMON/BROCCOLI CASSEROLE
Leta Tobin, Mabton, Washington

1 can (7-1/2 ounces) canned salmon
1 package (10 ounces) frozen chopped broccoli
1/3 cup chopped onion
1 tablespoon butter
1 can (10-3/4 ounces) cream of celery soup, undiluted
2 tablespoons lemon juice
1 egg, beaten
1/4 cup grated Parmesan cheese
1/2 teaspoon dried dill weed
1/8 teaspoon pepper
1-1/2 cups seasoned croutons *or* 1 cup dried bread crumbs
1 can (8 ounces) mushrooms, undrained

Drain salmon, reserving liquid. Remove skin and bones. Break into chunks; set aside. Cook broccoli according to package directions; drain. Saute onion in butter. Add soup; heat thoroughly. Stir in lemon juice, egg, cheese, dill weed, pepper, mushrooms and reserved salmon liquid. Blend in salmon, broccoli and croutons/bread crumbs; place in buttered shallow baking dish. Bake at 325° 20 minutes. Garnish with lemon slices. **Yield:** 4-6 servings.

CRUNCHY BROCCOLI/ BEAN CASSEROLE

Connie Bolton, San Antonio, Texas

2 packages (10 ounces each)
   chopped frozen broccoli
1 package (10 ounces) frozen
   baby lima beans
SAUCE:
1 can (10-3/4 ounces) cream
   of mushroom soup,
   undiluted
8 ounces dairy sour cream
1 package dry onion soup mix
1 can (6-1/2 ounces) water
   chestnuts, chopped
TOPPING:
1/2 cup butter, melted
3 cups crisp rice cereal

Cook broccoli and beans separately, following package directions; drain. Line 2-qt. or 3-qt. casserole dish with vegetable mixture. Combine sauce ingredients; spread over vegetable layer. Mix together butter and cereal; sprinkle over all. Bake at 325° for 30 minutes. **Yield:** 8-10 servings.

BROCCOLI AND SWEET PEPPER STIR-FRY

Karen Collin, Lethbridge, Alberta

1 pound fresh broccoli,
   washed and drained
1 sweet red pepper
1 sweet yellow pepper
1 tablespoon vegetable oil
   plus more as needed
1 onion, chopped
1 teaspoon grated fresh
   gingerroot *or* 1/4 teaspoon
   ground ginger
1/4 cup chicken stock
2 teaspoons soy sauce

Cut broccoli stems into crosswise slices 1/4 in. thick and florets into 1-in. pieces. Seed peppers; cut into thin strips. In large heavy skillet or wok, heat oil over medium heat. Add onion and ginger; stir-fry 1 minute. Add broccoli, peppers and more oil if needed; stir-fry 2-3 minutes. Add chicken stock; sprinkle with soy sauce. Serve at once. **Yield:** 8 servings.

DON'T WASTE A BIT OF BROCCOLI: Make the most of all parts of broccoli—peel the stalks of tougher stems and slice inner parts into thin bias cuts…then cook along with florets.

• Or, use edible stems in a casserole—chop or slice stems crosswise in 1/8-in. slices. Parboil in salted water for 6 to 7 minutes. Drain; pour into a shallow 1-1/2 qt. baking dish. Stir in 1 can (10-3/4 oz.) cream of celery soup and top with a mixture of 2 tablespoons crushed butter crackers and 2 tablespoons of finely shredded sharp cheddar cheese. Bake at 450° for 10-15 minutes.

BROCCOLI/CHEESE SOUP

Beth Fugate, Tazewell, Tennessee

1 cup water
1 chicken bouillon cube
1 package (10 ounces) frozen
   chopped broccoli
1 medium carrot, grated
2 to 3 tablespoons butter
3 tablespoons flour
2 cups milk
1 pound processed American
   cheese, cubed
1 can (10-3/4 ounces) cream
   of chicken soup, undiluted
1 tablespoon minced
   onion flakes
1 tablespoon Worcestershire
   sauce
Pepper to taste

Heat water and bouillon cube to boiling. Add broccoli and carrot; cook 5 minutes or until tender. Remove from heat; do not drain. In separate saucepan, melt butter; slowly stir in flour. Gradually add milk; cook until thickened. Stir in cheese, soup, onion, sauce and pepper. Add broccoli/carrot mixture; heat and serve. **Yield:** 10-12 servings.

FRESH RASPBERRY CAKE

Margery Peterson, Nyssa, Oregon

(PICTURED ON PAGE 40)

1 white cake mix
FILLING:
1 package (8 ounces) cream
   cheese
1 cup confectioners' sugar
1 cup whipping cream, whipped
1/2 cup confectioners' sugar

---

1 package (3-3/4 ounces)
   Raspberry Danish Dessert*
2 to 3 cups fresh raspberries

Prepare cake mix according to package directions and *remove 2 cups batter* before baking. Bake in greased and floured 13-in. x 9-in. x 2-in. pan at 350° until done. (Use remaining batter for cupcakes.) Set aside to cool. Mix cream cheese and 1 cup confectioners' sugar; fold in whipped cream combined with 1/2 cup of confectioners' sugar. Spread filling on cool cake and chill in refrigerator. Mix Danish Dessert with 1-1/2 cups cold water; cook as directed. Cool. Add fresh raspberries to cooled Danish Dessert; spread over filling layer on cake. Refrigerate overnight. *If Danish Dessert is unavailable, make sauce from 2 packages (10 oz. *each*) frozen raspberries, undrained. Crush raspberries in juice; strain through sieve to remove seeds. Place juice in saucepan and combine with 1/2 cup sugar and 2 tablespoons cornstarch; cook until clear. Chill. Proceed with recipe. **Yield:** 16 servings.

RASPBERRY GLACE PIE/TART

Elizabeth Karr, Tacoma, Washington

(PICTURED ON PAGE 40)

CRUST:
1/2 cup butter, softened
1/4 cup confectioners' sugar
1/2 teaspoon vanilla
1 cup flour
1/8 teaspoon salt
1/2 cup chopped nuts
FILLING:
1 quart fresh raspberries,
   rinsed gently and drained,
   divided
1 cup water, *divided*
3 tablespoons cornstarch
1 cup sugar

For crust, cream together butter, sugar and vanilla; add flour, salt and nuts (I prefer walnuts). Chill in bowl 30-40 minutes. Press into *deep* 9-in. pie plate or 8-in. tart pan. Bake at 400° for 10-12 minutes or until golden brown. Cool. For filling, simmer *1 cup berries with 2/3 cup water* for 3 minutes or until berries are soft. Strain out seeds and pulp. Blend remaining water, cornstarch and sugar; stir into berry mixture and continue cooking until thickened. Cool. Place remaining berries in baked crust; pour cooled glaze over all. Chill 2 hours or until set. Garnish with whipped cream, if desired. **Yield:** 8 servings.

CHERRIES 'N' CREAM ROLL

Mrs. John Nolt, Lititz, Pennsylvania

(PICTURED ON PAGE 40)

SPONGE CAKE:
- 1 cup cake flour
- 1 teaspoon baking powder
- 1/4 teaspoon salt
- 3 eggs
- 3/4 cup sugar
- 1 tablespoon frozen orange juice concentrate
- 2 tablespoons water

FILLING:
- 2 cups heavy cream, whipped
- 1/2 cup confectioners' sugar
- 1/2 teaspoon almond extract
- 1 can (21 ounces) cherry pie filling (*or* other fruit filling)

Grease a 15-in. x 10-in. x 1-in. jelly roll pan and line with waxed paper or parchment. Sift together flour, baking powder and salt; set aside. Beat eggs at high speed until thick; add sugar and beat until smooth and lemon-colored. Blend in orange concentrate and water at low speed; add dry ingredients slowly. *Do not overbeat.* Pour batter in pan and bake at 375° for 12 minutes. Invert cake onto a clean towel that has been liberally sprinkled with confectioners' sugar. Whip cream; add sugar and almond extract. Spread cooled cake with half of whipped cream and three-fourths of cherry filling. Roll up carefully. Frost with remaining whipped cream and cherry filling. Chill before serving. **Yield:** 10-12 servings.

DELICATE LEMON SQUARES

Ruby Nelson, Mountain Home, Arkansas

(PICTURED ON PAGE 40)

CRUST:
- 1 cup all-purpose flour
- 1/4 cup confectioners' sugar
- 1/2 cup butter

FILLING:
- 2 eggs
- 3/4 cup granulated sugar
- 3 tablespoons fresh lemon juice
- 2 tablespoons all-purpose flour

- 1/2 teaspoon baking powder
- Confectioners' sugar

Stir together flour and confectioners' sugar; cut in butter until mixture clings together. Pat into an ungreased 8-in. x 8-in. x 2-in. baking pan; bake at 350° for 10-12 minutes. Meanwhile, beat eggs in mixing bowl; add granulated sugar and lemon juice and beat until thick and smooth, 8-10 minutes. Stir together flour and baking powder; add to egg mixture, blending until all ingredients are moistened. Pour egg mixture gently over baked crust layer. Bake at 350° for 20-25 minutes. Cool slightly. Sift confectioners' sugar over top. Cool completely; cut cookies into 1-1/2-in. squares. **Yield:** about 3 dozen bars.

BUTTERFLIES

Marianne Robinson, Valencia, Pennsylvania

(PICTURED ON PAGE 40)

- 1 cup butter, chilled
- 1-1/2 cups all-purpose flour
- 1/2 cup dairy sour cream
- 1 teaspoon grated lemon peel
- About 3/4 cup granulated sugar

Cut butter and flour together; stir in sour cream and lemon peel. Shape into a 4-1/2-in. square; place on waxed paper and refrigerate 2 hours. Cut dough into four pieces; work with *one piece of dough at a time.* Sprinkle 2 tablespoons sugar on wax paper surface; coat dough in sugar. Roll dough into a 12-in. x 5-in. rectangle, flipping often. (Do not re-roll dough scraps.) On 12-in. edge, mark center. From each short end, roll dough to center mark. Wrap rolls and refrigerate 2 hours. Cut chilled rolls into 3/8-in. slices. Dip each slice into sugar on both sides. Bake on foil-lined baking sheets at 375° for 12-15 minutes or until golden brown. Turn over; bake 3 minutes more. Cool on wire rack. **Yield:** 40 cookies.

STRAWBERRY/KIWI TARTS

Becky Duncan, Leming, Texas

(PICTURED ON PAGE 41)

CRUST:
- 1 cup flour
- 1/2 cup confectioners' sugar
- 1/2 cup butter

CREAM FILLING:
- 1 package (8 ounces) cream cheese

- 1/2 cup sugar
- 1/4 teaspoon fresh lemon juice

TOPPING:
- 1 pint fresh strawberries, washed, stemmed and mashed
- 4 tablespoons sugar
- 1 tablespoon cornstarch
- 2 kiwis, peeled and sliced crosswise
- 1 pint fresh strawberries, washed, drained, sliced

For crust, combine flour and sugar; cut in butter until mixture clings together. Pat dough into single-serving tart forms (2 tablespoons each in about 19 shallow forms) *or* 12-in. pizza pan. Bake at 325° for about 10-15 minutes or until golden brown. Cool. For filling, combine cream cheese, sugar and lemon juice; beat until smooth and spread over pastry. Refrigerate. For topping, cook mashed strawberries over medium heat until juice is bright red; strain to remove pulp. Add sugar and cornstarch to strawberry juice; cook, stirring constantly, until thick. Cool. Spread thickened juice over cream cheese mixture; top with sliced strawberries and kiwis. Chill for 1-2 hours before serving. **Yield:** 10 servings *or* about 19 individual tarts.

MOM'S CREAM CHEESE MINTS

Alice Sunseri, St. Louis Park, Minnesota

(PICTURED ON PAGE 41)

- 4 ounces cream cheese, softened
- Confectioners' sugar
- Peppermint extract, about 1/4 teaspoon *or* to taste
- Wintergreen extract, about 1/4 teaspoon *or* to taste
- Green food coloring
- Red food coloring
- Granulated sugar

Mix cream cheese and confectioners' sugar by hand until smooth and doughy. Divide mixture in half; add a few drops of peppermint extract to one half and a few drops of wintergreen extract to other half. Taste and adjust flavor. Blend green food coloring (several drops at a time) into peppermint mixture until soft green; blend red food coloring (several drops at a time) into wintergreen mixture until pastel pink. Pinch off small pieces of dough; roll into balls and dip into granulated sugar. (Mints pictured have been pressed in various candy molds.) Refrigerate, covered. **Yield:** about 7 dozen mints.

WEDDING PUNCH

Marybeth Curran, Waukesha, Wisconsin

(PICTURED ON PAGE 41)

2 cans (12 ounces each) frozen lemonade concentrate
2 cans (12 ounces each) frozen pineapple juice concentrate
1 quart water
1 liter bottle ginger ale
1 liter bottle sparkling water
1 large bottle sparkling white grape juice *or* champagne
Fresh strawberries
Mint leaves

Combine juices and water in a large punch bowl; mix well. Right before serving, add ginger ale, sparkling water and juice/champagne. Stir to blend. Garnish glasses with fresh strawberries and a sprig of mint. (Freeze some of juice mixture in a pretty mold to keep punch cool without diluting flavors.) **Yield:** About 50 half-cup servings (4 ounces each).

IDAHO CHEF'S SALAD

Gladys DeBoer, Castleford, Idaho

(PICTURED ON PAGE 42)

2 cups Great Northern beans, cooked and drained
1 cup thin-sliced celery
Freshly ground black pepper

CHIVE DRESSING:
1/2 cup evaporated milk
1/2 cup vegetable oil
3 tablespoons cider vinegar
2 tablespoons chopped chives, fresh *or* freeze-dried
1 teaspoon salt
1 teaspoon white sugar
1/2 teaspoon dry mustard
1/4 teaspoon ground pepper
Chilled salad greens
4 ounces ham, slivered *or* julienne cuts
4 ounces Swiss cheese, slivered *or* julienne cuts
4 ounces cheddar cheese, slivered *or* julienne cuts
4 ounces cooked chicken *or* turkey, slivered *or* julienne cuts
3 hard-boiled eggs, sliced

Place beans in a large salad bowl; stir in celery and fresh ground pepper. Combine dressing ingredients; pour over beans until coated. Chill. Just before serving, tuck crisp salad greens around edges of bowl; arrange ham, cheeses and chicken on top of bean/celery mixture. Garnish with egg slices. **Yield:** 8 servings.

SPINACH CHICKEN SALAD

Kim Roe, Ventura, California

(PICTURED ON PAGE 42)

6 cups fresh spinach, stemmed, washed, drained and torn in bite-sized pieces
3 chicken breasts, boned and skinned
1 avocado, pitted and sliced
1 can (8 ounces) crushed pineapple, drained
1 small bunch green onions, cut into 1/4-inch slices
1 red *or* green pepper, chopped
2 cups alfalfa sprouts, rinsed, drained and chilled
1/2 cup toasted sunflower seeds
Buttermilk dressing

Place prepared spinach in a deep glass bowl; chill. Season chicken breasts as desired and cook in microwave or broiler until done; cool and cut into bite-sized pieces. Toss together spinach, chicken, avocado, pineapple, onions and pepper. Garnish with sprouts and sprinkle with sunflower seeds. Serve with buttermilk dressing. **Yield:** 6 servings.

PASTA PICNIC SALAD

Shirley Ramsey, Wymore, Nebraska

(PICTURED ON PAGE 42)

2 cups rotini pasta, uncooked
1 package (3-1/2 ounces) sliced pepperoni
2 avocados, peeled, sliced into small chunks, sprinkled with lemon juice
2 cups sliced fresh mushrooms
2 cups cherry tomatoes, halved
1/4 cup sliced green onions
1/4 teaspoon lemon pepper
3/4 cup bottled Italian salad dressing

Cook pasta according to package directions. Rinse with cold water; drain well. Combine with remaining ingredients, mixing gently but thoroughly. Cover; chill 4 hours or overnight. **Yield:** 6 servings.

ARTICHOKE RICE SALAD

Virginia Shaw, Modesto, California

(PICTURED ON PAGE 42)

3 cups long grain rice, cooked and drained
1 jar (14-3/4 ounces) marinated artichokes, *undrained*, chopped
1/2 cup coarsely chopped red bell pepper
1/4 cup sliced ripe olives
3 tablespoons minced fresh basil, optional
2 tablespoons minced red onion
2 tablespoons minced fresh parsley
DRESSING:
1/2 cup olive oil
3 tablespoons white wine vinegar
1/2 teaspoon Dijon mustard
1 clove garlic, minced
1/4 teaspoon salt
1/4 teaspoon pepper
1/3 cup toasted pine nuts *or* unsalted sunflower seeds

In large bowl, combine rice, artichokes, pepper, olives, basil, onion and parsley; toss gently until well blended. Combine dressing ingredients; mix well. Blend thoroughly into rice mixture. Right before serving, stir in nuts/seeds. Salad may be served immediately or chilled overnight. **Yield:** 10 servings.

OVEN-BAKED RICE IS NICE! This easy oven method for cooking rice is a never-fail way to have perfect rice every time! Start by placing 1 cup of uncooked long grain rice in a 1-1/2-quart baking dish. Stir in 2 cups boiling water and 1 teaspoon salt. Bake, covered, at 350° for 30 minutes, or until all liquid is absorbed. Cooked rice keeps well in the refrigerator for 4 to 5 days if tightly covered. It can also be frozen and will keep safely for about 6 months.

Flavorful variations: Try breakfast rice cooked in a combination of water and apple, pineapple or orange juice. Serve with brown sugar, cinnamon, nutmeg or grated orange peel, or stir in nuts, raisins, honey or crumbled bacon.

● For a suppertime side dish, use a combination of water and chicken or beef broth or of water and tomato juice. Season cooked rice with curry, dill, saffron, parsley, ginger, basil, garlic or paprika. Stir in shredded carrot, cooked mushrooms, lemon juice, diced onions or green peppers for variety.

BEST COOK

For many of our "Best Cooks" the pleasure of cooking well seems secondary to satisfying others with hearty, wholesome food. That's certainly true of Ruthe Stevenson of Minneapolis, Minnesota.

Ruthe has cooked at the Mt. Olivet-Careview Nursing Home for nearly 13 years. But when she takes her summer vacation, she doesn't let someone else cook for her—she spends 2 weeks cooking at a church camp!

Jeannette Butler, who nominated Ruthe, writes, "She was one of the first campers when the Big Stone Camp for Christ opened in 1947, and over the years she's seen the facilities improve from a few tents to modern cabins, washrooms and a dining hall.

"For the past 9 years, Ruthe has expressed her deep love and loyalty to the camp by using her vacation to cook for us. She's a real favorite, as you can see by the petition I've enclosed—signed by 100 campers and staff members! Ruthe is loved by all, because she loves everybody."

"My dearest pleasure," Ruthe told us, "is to serve something from my kitchen and have people say, 'Boy, is this great!' Cooking for my friends at the nursing home and those at the camp is really rewarding because I can warm their tummies as well as their hearts!"

OVEN BARBECUED RIBS

3 to 4 pounds country style ribs
1 large onion, thinly sliced

SAUCE:
    1 cup catsup
   1/3 cup Worcestershire sauce
    1 teaspoon chili powder
    1 teaspoon salt
1-1/2 cups water

Place ribs in 13-in. x 9-in. x 2-in. baking pan. Bake at 450° for 30 minutes; drain off fat. Cover ribs with onion slices. Combine sauce ingredients; bring to boil. Pour sauce over ribs/onions. Reduce oven to 350°; bake, uncovered, 1-1/2 hours. Baste with sauce every 15 minutes. Add more water to sauce if sauce becomes too dry. **Yield:** 3-4 servings.

BROWN BREAD

    2 cups water
    1 cup chopped dates
    2 teaspoons baking soda
1/2 cup butter, room temperature
    2 cups sugar
    2 eggs, room temperature
    2 teaspoons vanilla
    4 cups all-purpose flour

Bring water, dates and baking soda to boil; cool. Meanwhile, cream butter and sugar together until smooth and light. Add eggs one at a time, beating after each addition. Add vanilla; stir to blend. Stir in cooled date/water mixture. Mix in flour until blended. Stir to blend. Fill well-greased 16 ounce cans about one-half full of batter. Bake at 350° for 1 hour. (Fill cans evenly for ease in timing bread.) **Yield:** 6-7 breads.

COCONUT CHOCOLATE CHIP COOKIES

    1 cup butter
    1 cup brown sugar
    1 cup granulated sugar
    2 eggs
    2 tablespoons water
    1 teaspoon baking soda
1/2 teaspoon salt
    1 teaspoon vanilla
    2 cups old fashioned oats
    1 cup coconut
    2 cups all-purpose flour

    1 package (6 ounces)
    semisweet chocolate chips

Cream together butter, sugars, eggs and water into a very smooth dough. Mix in remaining ingredients until blended. Drop on ungreased cookie sheets about 1 inch apart. Bake at 375° for 10-12 minutes or until golden brown. **Yield:** About 6-1/2 dozen 2-1/2-inch cookies.

RUTHE'S FAVORITE FROSTING

3 heaping tablespoons creamy
  peanut butter
3 heaping tablespoons butter,
  soft but not melted
1 teaspoon vanilla
2 cups powdered sugar
3 heaping tablespoons cocoa
1/8 teaspoon salt
2 to 4 tablespoons milk plus
  additional as needed

Mix together peanut butter, butter and vanilla. Stir in powdered sugar, cocoa and salt. Add milk, stirring until you reach desired spreading consistency. Use on your favorite layer cake or cupcakes.

GOING THROUGH A STAGE: If you don't have a candy thermometer handy, use these quick tests to determine the temperature of sugar syrup mixtures:

Thread Stage (230°-233°)—syrup runs from a spoon into a 2-in. fine thread.

Soft-Ball Stage (234°-240°)—a small amount of syrup dropped into cold water forms a ball that, when removed from water, flattens immediately and runs between your fingers.

Firm-Ball Stage (244°-248°)—a small amount of syrup dropped into cold water forms a ball that holds its shape but flattens quickly at room temperature.

Hard-Ball Stage (250°-266°)—a small amount of syrup dropped into cold water forms a ball that can be deformed by pressure but will not flatten.

Soft-Crack Stage (270°-290°)—a small amount of syrup dropped into cold water will separate into hard but pliable threads.

Hard-Crack Stage (295°-310°)—a small amount of syrup dropped into cold water will separate into hard, brittle threads that snap easily.

COUNTRY INNS

The Inn at Cedar Falls

21190 State Route 374, Logan, Ohio 43138

Phone: 1-614/385-7489

Directions: From Columbus, Ohio take U.S. 33 south to Rte. 664, right 9-1/2 mi. to Rte. 374, left 1 mile to inn.

Innkeepers: Anne Castle and Ellen Grinsfelder, Debra Coyan and Karen Ness.

Schedule: Open year-round. Restaurant closed Sundays.

Accommodations and Rates: Nine rooms with private baths, $57-$75 double occupancy, $45-$60 single occupancy, with full breakfast. Dinners by reservation, $17-$25 per person. Smoking restricted. One ground-floor room planned to accommodate handicapped guests.

The kitchen's open at the Inn at Cedar Falls—in more ways than one. Though innkeeper Anne Castle does most of the cooking, once a month she invites a guest chef to take over making dinner. And whether she's in the kitchen or a guest chef is at the range, the people staying at the inn are welcome to watch them cook, sample the upcoming dishes or even help make jams, jellies and chutneys in the roomy, country-style kitchen.

A guest chef may dish up Caesar salad topped with tuna croutons and daylily blossoms fried in a spicy batter. Next comes grilled, marinated chicken breasts, complemented by sauteed peaches with country ham as a main course...and a dream dessert of Chocolate Raspberry Gavache Torte with raspberry sauce.

Breakfast, served outside on sunny days, might include this French toast —stuffed with cream cheese and preserves, served with crisp bacon and orange juice.

The next evening, enjoy Anne's handiwork, in a dinner menu that's simple but enjoyable—tomato-dill soup, garden salad, pasta primavera, warm biscuits and ginger muffins, followed by dessert of peach and raspberry Clafouti. (By the way, this dessert is marvelous using whatever combination of fruits that's in season— such as apples with walnuts or pears with pecans.)

FANCY FRENCH TOAST

> 1 loaf French bread
> 12 ounces cream cheese
> 1/3 cup peach preserves (or flavor of your choice)
> 10 eggs
> 2-1/2 cups milk
> 1/2 teaspoon cinnamon
> Dash nutmeg
> 1 teaspoon vanilla
> Butter

Slice French bread into 20 1-inch-thick pieces. Slice two-thirds through each piece of bread, making a pocket. Mix cream cheese and preserves; fill each pocket with a generous tablespoon of the mixture. Beat together eggs, milk, seasonings and vanilla. Dip each slice of bread in the egg mixture and fry in melted butter until golden brown. Serve with maple syrup. **Yield:** 10 servings.

PEACH AND RASPBERRY CLAFOUTI

> 4 cups peaches (about 2-1/2 pounds), thickly sliced
> 1/2 cup raspberries
> 2 tablespoons cold, unsalted butter, cut into bits
> 1/4 cup blanched almonds
> 2 tablespoons flour
> 3/4 cup heavy cream *or* half-and-half *or* milk
> 1/3 cup plus 2 tablespoons sugar
> 2 large eggs
> 1 tablespoon tawny red port *or* sherry, optional
> 1/4 teaspoon salt
> 1 cup whipped cream
> Raspberries, mint leaves to garnish

Layer peaches and raspberries in a buttered, shallow 5-cup baking dish; dot with butter. In blender or food processor, grind almonds with flour. Add cream, 1/3 cup sugar, eggs, port, salt; blend, scraping sides as necessary. Pour custard slowly over fruit. Sprinkle top with 2 tablespoons sugar. Bake at 400° for 30 to 40 minutes until top is golden and custard set. Cool on rack for 20 minutes. Serve warm with whipped cream, garnished with raspberries and mint. **Yield:** 8 servings.

HEARTY BEEF STEW

> 2 pounds stewing beef, cut in 1-inch cubes
> Flour, salt and pepper
> Cooking oil
> Dash each Worcestershire sauce, hot pepper sauce and garlic powder
> 1 large onion, chopped
> 1 cup beef bouillon
> 1/2 cup dry red wine
> 1 large can tomatoes, quartered
> 12 peppercorns
> 3 whole cloves
> 2 bay leaves
> 1/4 cup chopped parsley
> 2-3 carrots, pared and sliced diagonally
> 5 medium new potatoes, quartered
> 4 ounces bite-sized mushrooms
> 1 jar small onions, drained
> 1 cup frozen green peas, defrosted
> Salt and pepper to taste

Dredge stew meat in flour, salt and pepper; brown in cooking oil. Sprinkle with seasonings. Add next 9 ingredients, simmer 3-4 hours until meat is tender. (You may want to do this step in the morning and let the stew sit until you finish it for dinner.) Half an hour before serving, cook potatoes until almost tender and add to stew. During the last 5 minutes of cooking, add the mushrooms, onions, green peas and salt and pepper. **Yield:** 7 servings.

VEGETABLE VIEWS: Buy mushrooms before they "open." When stems and caps are attached snugly, mushrooms are truly fresh.

● To cook "below the ground" vegetables, such as potatoes, carrots and turnips, place in cold water and bring to a boil. Add "above the ground" vegetables—corn, peas, beans—to water that's already boiling.

● To keep celery crisp, stand it up in a pitcher of cold, salted water and refrigerate.

● Lettuce keeps better if you store it in the refrigerator without washing it, so the leaves are dry. Wash just before using.

BEST COOK

Most of the "Best Cook in the Country" winners have been nominated by a family member or close friend. But Bonnie Ziegler of Rincon, Georgia, was nominated by a committee!

A letter signed by 44 fellow workers at the Skidway Institute of Oceanography read in part, "Bonnie arrives early each day, and as the rest of us come in, we stop by her office to see if she's brought homemade 'treats.' We always look forward to birthdays and special occasions, since Bonnie is sure to bring her luscious fresh coconut pound cake.

"Bonnie often organizes covered dish lunches. Somehow she finds time to bring such crowd-pleasers as fresh cut creamed corn, butter beans or fried corn bread—enough to feed 40 people!

"Occasionally we persuade Bonnie to bring her potato-onion soup, made with vegetables from her garden. The aroma from the slow-cooker fills the hallways, and we can't wait to gather in her office at noon to enjoy the generous portions she ladles out.

"Each of us admires the energy of this remarkable woman. In addition to her job, Bonnie's involved in many family and church activities. She and her husband plant a 2-acre garden and her front yard has over 600 azaleas!

"Bonnie shares much more than fine food. She's an example for us all

with her positive attitude, her giving nature, and her engaging smile!"

And Bonnie bubbled with enthusiasm when we talked to her.

"I have been cooking since I was 9, and I've always loved it," she said. "I especially enjoy baking for our church socials, and I've had plenty of opportunities—we often hold bake sales.

"Each year I also can many, many jars of fruit, vegetables, jam, jellies, preserves and pickles. It's fun sharing my canned goods with co-workers."

FRESH COCONUT POUND CAKE

- **1 cup butter, softened**
- **3 cups sugar**
- **6 eggs**
- **3 cups all-purpose flour**
- **1/4 teaspoon baking soda**
- **1/4 teaspoon salt**
- **1 carton (8 ounces) dairy sour cream**
- **1 cup fresh (*or* frozen, thawed) coconut**
- **1 teaspoon vanilla extract**
- **1 teaspoon coconut extract**
ICING:
- **1/2 cup vegetable shortening**
- **1 pound box of confectioners' sugar**
- **1/4 cup water**
- **1/8 teaspoon salt**
- **1 teaspoon vanilla**

Cream together butter and sugar; beat until mixture is light and fluffy. Add one egg at a time, beating well after each addition. Combine flour, soda and salt. Mix well; add to creamed mixture alternately with sour cream, beginning and ending with flour mixture. Stir in the coconut and both flavorings. Pour batter into a greased and floured 10-in. tube pan. Bake at 350° for 1 hour and 20 minutes or until a wooden pick inserted in the center comes out clean. Cool in pan 10-15 minutes; remove from pan and cool completely before icing or cutting. To make icing, combine all ingredients in large bowl and mix at high speed until fluffy. Frost top and sides. **Yield:** 16 servings.

GRILLED FLANK STEAK

- **1-1/2 pounds flank steak (cut as thick as possible)**
- **1 teaspoon dry basil leaves**
- **1 package (6 ounces) sliced hard salami**
- **1 small white onion, thinly sliced**
- **1 package (6 ounces) sliced provolone cheese**

Place flank steak in freezer until firm enough to make a pocket (you can do a better job of making a pocket in steak when it's slightly frozen). Lay flank steak flat. With a sharp knife, carefully slice along one of long edges to make a horizontal pocket almost as big as the steak. *Be careful not to cut through at sides or back.* Open pocket; sprinkle inside evenly with basil. Layer one-half of salami on bottom of pocket, all of onions slices, cheese and remaining one-half of salami. Use wooden skewers or wooden toothpicks to close the opening. Place steak flat on grill 4-6 inches above a bed of medium coals. Cook 7-8 minutes on each side for medium rare—longer or shorter depending on doneness desired. When done, place on carving board. Cut across grain of meat in slanting slices about 1/2-inch thick. Serve immediately. **Yield:** 4-6 servings.

POTATO SOUP

- **5 pounds new red potatoes, scrubbed and diced**
- **1-1/4 cups butter**
- **2 large minced onions, about 2 cups**
- **4 stalks celery, minced**
- **2 cloves garlic, minced**
- **4 tablespoons all-purpose flour**
- **1 pound mild cheddar cheese, grated**
- **1 quart half-and-half**
- **1 pint whole milk**
Salt to taste
Pepper to taste

Cook potatoes in large kettle with enough water to cover until they begin to boil. Turn off heat; leave kettle on burner, covered. Saute onions, celery and garlic in butter in large skillet until vegetables are transparent. Add flour; stir well. Add to potatoes and water; stir well. Add grated cheese; stir to melt. Add half-and-half and milk. Add salt and pepper to taste. DO NOT LET MIXTURE BOIL. **Yield:** 25 servings.

It's the time to move meals outdoors again—no matter where you're heading. Whether your summertime fare's being served off the tailgate of a pickup or at a more leisurely pace from a picnic table in the park, you'll find two hidden ingredients in these recipes that you'll be glad to discover! All these outdoor-oriented recipes emphasize easy eating and quick cleanup, so the cook can get out and enjoy the season, too.

HEARTY HARVEST HELPINGS: Clockwise from lower left—**Summer Sauerkraut Salad,** Karen Ann Bland, Gove, Kansas (Pg. 59); **Perfect Picnic Basket,** Maralynn Lindstrom, Spring, Texas (Pg. 59); **Spicy Sandwich Loaf,** Judy Smith, Winthrop, Maine (Pg. 60); **Old-Fashioned Lemonade,** Laura Helmuth, Nappanee, Indiana (Pg. 60); **Marinated Tomatoes,** Katie Dreibelbis, Santa Clara, California (Pg. 60); **Sour Cream Chocolate Sheet Cake,** Janet Tigchelaar, Jerseyville, Ontario (Pg. 60); **Oriental Chicken Cabbage Salad,** Lonnie Heimer, Fort Collins, Colorado (Pg. 60); **Banana Cake with Peanut Butter Icing,** Carolina Hofeldt, Lloyd, Montana (Pg. 59).

Pack a picnic basket with these dishes and you'll truly have a movable feast!

Start with Spicy Picnic Pasties, a tangier version of an ethnic favorite. Add Hearty Baked Potato Salad, a standout side dish you can serve hot or at "field temperature". And what picnic's complete without baked beans? This Six-Bean Casserole adds the hearty, spicy taste of Italian sausage as well.

For dessert, Soft Molasses Cookies are an old-fashioned favorite.

Take your meal to the field…or the park…or the beach to satisfy those fresh-air-whetted appetites!

EATING OUT—AT ITS BEST: Top to bottom—**Soft Molasses Cookies,** LaVonne Hegland, St. Michael, Minnesota; **Hearty Baked Potato Salad,** Mary Begtson-Almquist, Petersburg, Illinois; **Six-Bean Casserole,** Marsha Ransom, South Haven, Michigan; **Spicy Picnic Pasties,** Virginia Doyle, Pinedale, Wyoming. (All recipes can be found on page 61).

Recipes by Sheila Wyum, Rutland, North Dakota

MEALS IN MINUTES

HERE'S A PROMPT pork chop menu that satisfies hearty, meat-and-potatoes appetites—in less than 30 minutes!

Begin the meal preparation by mixing seasonal fresh fruit with a tangy dressing made from frozen limeade concentrate.

While the fruit salad chills, stir together the glaze ingredients and begin broiling or grilling the pork chops. Garden vegetables such as fresh peas are cooked in chicken bouillon, with slices of water chestnut added for extra crunch.

To round out the meal, frozen Southern-style hash browns are especially handy. Quickly cook them according to package directions to complete a satisfying and speedy supper.

ORANGE GLAZED PORK CHOPS

1/4 cup grated onion
1 tablespoon butter
2 tablespoons brown sugar
1-1/2 teaspoons cornstarch
1/2 teaspoon ground ginger
1 cup orange juice
1 tablespoon bottled steak sauce
6 pork chops, 1-inch-thick cuts

Combine glaze ingredients and cook in microwave or on stovetop until thick. Broil or grill pork chops 5-7 minutes per side (or until the juices run clear), basting with glaze as meat cooks. **Yield:** 6 servings.

PEAS WITH WATER CHESTNUTS

1 package (10 ounces) frozen peas *or* 2 cups fresh garden peas
4 ounces sliced water chestnuts
1 can (10-3/4 ounces) chicken broth *or* 1 teaspoon instant chicken bouillon granules dissolved in 1 cup water

1 tablespoon butter
Pinch of salt and sugar, if desired

Simmer peas and water chestnuts in chicken broth about 5 minutes or until peas are done. Add butter and seasonings, if desired. **Yield:** 4 servings.

FRESH FRUIT SALAD WITH LIMEADE DRESSING

2 bananas, sliced
1 cup green seedless grapes
1 cup whole strawberries
Watermelon or cantaloupe chunks
2 tablespoons frozen limeade concentrate, thawed (add additional to taste)

Place fruit in bowl. Pour on undiluted limeade, stir gently. **Yield:** 4 servings.

FOILED AGAIN! Take along a roll of heavy-duty aluminum foil. With it, you can...line the grill for reflected heat and quick, neat disposal of ashes...form drip pans in whatever shape you need ...shape a portable windbreak for the fire...make your own warming oven... enclose vegetables for on-the-grill cooking...wrap freshly caught fish for transportation home...make cups for holding basting sauces...line a wheelbarrow before filling it with ice for watermelon or cantaloupe slices or bottles or cans of soda.

GRILLING HINTS: A spray bottle filled with water will quickly douse flare-ups in the charcoal grill. Also remember to pack a basting brush for marinades and sauces, tongs for turning and serving grilled foods, reclosable plastic bags for leftovers and/or dirty utensils and a garbage bag for trash.

Bring a hankerin'...and *a dish to pass.* That's how the notice reads, and it's your invitation to some classic country eating—at an old-fashioned potluck dinner in the church basement or town hall.

Community cooks bring their best to buffets: tried-and-true recipes calculated to serve (and satisfy!) a crowd. Neighbors line up at the serving table, eyeing the offerings and helping themselves to delicious dishes, all the while hoping their favorite (always at the far end!) will last till they reach it.

The serving's starting, so take your plate, find a spot in line and enjoy these potluck recipes!

BLESSED BOUNTY: Clockwise on our buffet table from lower left—**Debbie's Deviled Eggs,** Debbie Lampert, Milton, Wisconsin (Pg. 62); **Company** Potatoes, James Gheduzi, Mt. Pleasant, Michigan (Pg. 62); **Adreana's Greek Pasta Salad,** Lee Souleles, Northridge, California (Pg. 62); **Spiced Chicken Wings,** Marion Stanley, Gilroy, California (Pg. 62); **Zesty Carrots,** James McMonagle, Bethel Park, Pennsylvania (Pg. 63); **Bibb Lettuce Salad,** Marcella Swigert, Monroe City, Missouri (Pg. 62); **Delaware Chicken Divan,** Joan Mills, Greenwood, Delaware (Pg. 62); **Cheeseburger Onion Pie,** Sharon Jakovac, Salmon, Idaho (Pg. 63).

No potluck would be complete without a fancy, fruit-flavored gelatin dessert such as the Red, White and Blue Salad below right.

And church-basement buffets are bound to boast great baked goods from pie makers and cake bakers proud to share their best. Treat your taste buds to their sweet favorites— old-time Chocolate Fudge Cake, taste-tempting Buttermilk Coconut Pie and unusually delicious Sour Cream Pear Pie. Come on, help yourself!

SWEETS TO SAVOR: Clockwise from lower left—**Sour Cream Pear Pie,** Susan Mason, Twin Falls, Idaho (Pg. 63); **Buttermilk Coconut Pie,** Marie Brown, Carthage, Mississippi (Pg. 64); **Chocolate Fudge Cake,** Pat Schaffer, Bark River, Michigan (Pg. 63); **Red, White and Blue Salad,** Jeannette Larson, Washington, D.C. (Pg. 64).

PERFECT PICNIC BASKET
Maralynn Lindstrom, Spring, Texas

(PICTURED ON PAGE 52)

COATING:
- 1/2 cup flour
- 1-1/2 tablespoons sesame seeds
- 1 teaspoon dried thyme
- 1/2 teaspoon dried tarragon
- 1/2 teaspoon poppy seeds
- 1 teaspoon salt
- 1/2 teaspoon pepper

- 3-1/2 pounds fryer chicken pieces, washed and drained
- 2 egg whites, lightly beaten
- 3 tablespoons butter
- 2 tablespoons margarine *or* vegetable oil

HERB SAUCE:
- 4 tablespoons butter, melted
- 3 tablespoons sesame seeds
- 1/2 teaspoon dried thyme
- 1/2 teaspoon dried tarragon
- 1/2 teaspoon garlic powder
- 1/2 teaspoon poppy seeds

- 1 large, round loaf of bread

Combine coating ingredients in a large plastic bag. Dip chicken pieces in egg whites and shake, a few at a time, in coating mixture. Heat butter and margarine/oil in large skillet; brown chicken over medium heat. Remove chicken to casserole dish; cover. Bake at 350° for 30 minutes. Combine the herb sauce ingredients. Slice top off bread and hollow out loaf with fork, leaving a 1/2-in.-thick shell. (Save the removed bread for croutons or crumbs.) Brush inside of hollowed loaf and top with herb sauce; place the loaf on baking sheet. Put baked chicken pieces inside hollowed loaf. Bake at 350° for 20 minutes. Remove; put lid on loaf. Serve warm. (To transport, wrap in foil and several layers of newspaper.) **Yield:** 4 servings.

BANANA CAKE WITH PEANUT BUTTER ICING
Carolina Hofeldt, Lloyd, Montana

(PICTURED ON PAGE 52)

CAKE:
- 2-1/4 cups all-purpose flour
- 1-1/4 teaspoons baking powder
- 1 teaspoon baking soda
- 1 teaspoon salt
- 1 cup mashed very ripe bananas (2 large)
- 1 cup buttermilk, room temperature

- 2/3 cup shortening
- 1-1/2 cups sugar
- 2 eggs, room temperature
- 1 teaspoon vanilla extract

ICING:
- 1 package (8 ounces) cream cheese, softened
- 1/2 cup light corn syrup
- 1/2 cup creamy peanut butter
- Chopped unsalted peanuts, about 1 cup

In a medium bowl, combine flour, baking powder, baking soda and salt; set aside. In a separate bowl, combine bananas and the buttermilk; set aside. Cream together shortening and sugar in large mixer bowl, beating until light and fluffy. Add eggs, one at a time, beating well after each addition. Beat in vanilla. Alternately add flour mixture and banana mixture, beginning and ending with flour. Beat until well blended. Spread evenly in a greased and floured 13-in. x 9-in. x 2-in. baking pan. Bake at 350° for 30 to 35 minutes or until wooden pick inserted in center comes out clean. Cool cake completely in pan on wire rack. To make icing, mix together cream cheese and corn syrup in small mixer bowl until smooth. Add peanut butter; beat until well-blended. Spread on cooled cake. Garnish with chopped peanuts. Refrigerate cake until serving time. **Yield:** 20 servings.

SUMMER SAUERKRAUT SALAD
Karen Ann Bland, Gove, Kansas

(PICTURED ON PAGE 52)

 This tasty dish uses less sugar, salt and fat. Recipe includes *Diabetic Exchanges*.

- 1 can (16 ounces) sauerkraut, drained and rinsed
- 1/2 cup red *or* green pepper, chopped fine
- 2 cups celery, chopped fine
- 1 small onion, chopped fine
- 1/2 cup sugar
- 1/4 teaspoon salt
- 1/8 teaspoon pepper

Combine all ingredients. Refrigerate until serving time. **Yield:** 10 servings. **Diabetic Exchanges:** One serving equals 2 vegetables, also; 54 calories, 424 mg sodium, 0 cholesterol, 14 gm carbohydrate, 1 gm protein, 0 fat.

CINNAMON CHEWS
Paula Johnson, Eaton, Colorado

- 1 pound marshmallows
- 1 package (9 ounces) red-hot cinnamon candies
- 3 tablespoons butter
- 1/2 teaspoon salt
- 2-1/2 cups crisp rice cereal
- Confectioners' sugar

Combine all ingredients but cereal and melt in top of double boiler. Add cereal, mixing quickly. Spread in buttered 8-in.-square pan. Chill; cut in 1-in. squares. Dust with powdered sugar. Wrap individually in waxed paper. **Yield:** 64 candies.

OUTDOOR EATING ADVICE: Keep summer salads and all chilled foods in coolers or insulated containers, covered and out of direct sunlight. Mayonnaise-based salads, hot dogs, lunch meats, cooked beef or chicken, deviled eggs and custard or cream pies will stay fresh for hours if kept cold.

MAMA'S STRAWBERRY CAKE
Diane O'Neal, Concord, California

CAKE:
- 1 package (18 ounces) white cake mix
- 3 tablespoons flour
- 1 package frozen strawberries, *divided*
- 4 eggs
- 1/2 cup vegetable oil
- 3/4 cup water
- 1 package (3 ounces) strawberry gelatin dessert

ICING:
- Half of frozen strawberries, reserved from cake
- 3-1/2 to 4 cups confectioners' sugar
- 1/2 cup butter

Combine cake ingredients in a large mixing bowl and beat 4 minutes on medium speed. Pour batter into two greased and floured 9-in. layer cake pans or into 13-in. x 9-in. x 2-in. pan. Bake at 350° for 30-35 minutes or until cake tests done. Cool in pans for 10 minutes; remove cake to wire rack and cool completely. Combine icing ingredients and mix until smooth and fluffy. Frost cool cake with the icing. Serve and store chilled. **Yield:** 16 servings.

MARINATED TOMATOES
Katie Dreibelbis, Santa Clara, California

(PICTURED ON PAGE 53)

✓ This tasty dish uses less sugar, salt and fat. Recipe includes *Diabetic Exchanges*.

6 large ripe red tomatoes
MARINADE:
1/4 cup green onions, sliced thinly
1/2 teaspoon dried thyme *or* 2 tablespoons fresh
1 clove garlic, minced fine
1/4 cup minced parsley
1 teaspoon salt
1/4 teaspoon freshly cracked black pepper
1/4 cup red *or* white vinegar
1/3 cup vegetable oil

Peel tomatoes and cut in 1/2-in.-thick slices; place in shallow dish. In separate bowl, combine the green onions, thyme, garlic, parsley, salt and pepper. Sprinkle mixture over tomatoes. Combine oil and vinegar in shaker; blend well. Pour over tomatoes. Cover; refrigerate at least 2 hours. Spoon marinade over tomatoes from time to time. **Yield:** 10 servings. **Diabetic Exchanges:** One serving equals 1 vegetable, 1-1/2 fats, also; 93 calories, 218 mg sodium, 0 cholesterol, 6 gm carbohydrate, 2 gm protein, 8 gm fat.

SPICY SANDWICH LOAF
Judy Smith, Winthrop, Maine

(PICTURED ON PAGE 53)

1 tablespoon butter
1 cup sliced mushrooms
1/2 cup chopped green pepper
1 pound frozen bread dough, thawed
1/4 pound thinly sliced ham
1/4 pound thinly sliced salami, casing removed
1/4 pound thinly sliced mozzarella *or* Provalone cheese
1-1/2 ounces thinly sliced pepperoni

Melt butter in a large skillet. Add mushrooms and green pepper; cook, stirring often, until tender. Set aside. On a large baking sheet lined with aluminum foil, press dough into a 10-in. x 13-in. rectangle. Layer ham, salami, cheese and pepperoni down center of dough; top with mushrooms and pepper. Fold sides of dough over filling, lapping the edges. Turn seam side

down; pinch ends together and tuck under to seal. Cover and let rise in warm place for 1 to 1-1/2 hours, until doubled in bulk. Brush with egg glaze, if desired. Bake at 350° for 45 minutes until golden brown. Let stand for 10 minutes before slicing. **Yield:** 8-10 servings.

ORIENTAL CHICKEN CABBAGE SALAD
Lonnie Heimer, Fort Collins, Colorado

(PICTURED ON PAGE 53)

1 whole chicken breast, cooked, cut and slivered *or* 2 cans (5 ounces each) canned white chicken meat
2 tablespoons toasted sesame seeds
2 ounces slivered toasted almonds
1/2 head cabbage, shredded fine
2 green onions, chopped fine
1 package (3 ounces) chicken-flavored Ramen noodles
SALAD DRESSING:
1/2 package Ramen noodle seasoning mix
3 tablespoons sugar
1/2 cup vegetable oil
3 tablespoons rice *or* wine vinegar
1 teaspoon salt
1/2 teaspoon pepper

Combine the chicken with seeds, almonds, cabbage, onion and *uncooked* noodles which have been broken apart. Add the dressing; toss to blend. Cover; refrigerate until serving time. Serve cold. **Yield:** 6 servings.

SOUR CREAM CHOCOLATE SHEET CAKE
Janet Tigchelaar, Jerseyville, Ontario

(PICTURED ON PAGE 53)

CAKE:
2 cups all-purpose flour
1 teaspoon baking soda
1/2 cup dairy sour cream
1 teaspoon salt
2 cups white sugar
3 eggs, beaten
1 cup butter
1 cup water
2 squares (2 ounces) unsweetened chocolate
ICING:
1/2 cup butter
1/3 cup milk

1 cup brown sugar
2 squares (2 ounces) chocolate
1 cup chopped nuts (walnuts are excellent)
1 cup confectioners' sugar
1 teaspoon vanilla

To make cake, combine flour, soda, sour cream, salt, sugar and beaten eggs in a large bowl. Mix until smooth; set aside. In a small saucepan, combine butter, water and chocolate; bring to a boil. Add chocolate mixture to batter; mix together very well. *Batter will be thin.* Pour batter into greased 17-in. x 11-1/2-in. x 1-in. jelly roll pan. Bake at 350° for 25 minutes. Cool in pan on wire rack. To make icing, combine butter, milk, brown sugar and chocolate in heavy saucepan. Bring to boil; *do not stir.* Boil for 3 minutes. Remove from heat; immediately stir in the nuts, sugar and vanilla. Pour hot icing onto center of cake; spread gently to outer edges. Cool and cut into squares. **Yield:** 40 squares, 2 inches each.

OUTDOOR EATING: Put "portable" foods in airtight plastic containers with see-through lids to make it easy to tell what's inside. ● Three- or four-section plastic plates are sturdier than paper plates and much less messy. ● Freeze single-serving juice cartons for an hour before you leave the house. They'll help chill food in coolers and thaw to a thirst-quenching slush by the time you get to the picnic or field.

OLD-FASHIONED LEMONADE
Laura Helmuth, Nappanee, Indiana

(PICTURED ON PAGE 53)

6 lemons
1-1/2 cups sugar
2-1/2 quarts ice water

Wash lemons; slice thin. Place in a stainless or enamel container. Add sugar. Pound with wooden spoon or mallet to squeeze juice from lemon rings; stir to make syrup. Let stand 20 minutes. Add ice water and 10 to 12 ice cubes; stir well. Serve within 6 hours for best flavors. **Yield:** 3 quarts.

HEARTY BAKED POTATO SALAD

Mary Bengtson-Almquist, Petersburg, Illinois

(PICTURED ON PAGE 54)

8 red salad potatoes
1/2 cup onion, chopped
2 tablespoons parsley, chopped
1 can (11 ounces) cheddar cheese soup
1/2 cup mayonnaise
1/2 cup plain yogurt
4 ounces bacon, cooked, drained and crumbled
Paprika for garnish

Peel potatoes; boil until soft. Cut in 1-1/2-in. chunks. Spread potatoes evenly over bottom of 13-in. x 9-in. x 2-in. baking pan. Combine onions, parsley, soup, mayonnaise and yogurt; pour over potatoes. Sprinkle cooked bacon on top; garnish with paprika. Cover with aluminum foil and bake at 350° for 1 hour, uncovering during the last 30 minutes. **Yield:** 10-12 servings.

SPICY PICNIC PASTIES

Virginia Doyle, Pinedale, Wyoming

(PICTURED ON PAGE 54)

PASTRY:
2 cups all-purpose flour
1/2 cup butter
1/2 teaspoon salt
6 to 7 tablespoons milk *or* as much as needed to make dough
FILLING:
3/4 pound ground beef
2 tablespoons chopped onion
1 tablespoon chopped bell pepper
1 to 2 tablespoons chopped celery
1/4 teaspoon ground cumin
1/4 to 1/2 teaspoon chili powder
1/2 teaspoon salt
2 tablespoons barbecue sauce

Combine pastry ingredients as for pie crust; divide dough into four parts. Roll each part thin and cut into a 6-in.-diameter circle, using a small plate as a guide. (If you prefer, substitute store-bought refrigerated pastry.) Combine filling ingredients. Place a fourth of filling in center of each dough circle; pat filling down lightly. Moisten edges of dough with water; fold circle in half to make a turnover. Seal edges well with a fork. Prick top to allow the steam to escape; place on an ungreased cookie

sheet. Bake at 375° for about 40 minutes. Serve—hot or cold—dipped in catsup, barbecue or chili sauce. **Yield:** 4 large servings.

SOFT MOLASSES COOKIES

LaVonne Hegland, St. Michael, Minnesota

(PICTURED ON PAGE 54)

1/2 cup butter, softened
1/2 cup solid vegetable shortening (not margarine)
1-1/2 cups sugar
1/2 cup molasses
2 eggs, lightly beaten
4 cups flour
1/2 teaspoon salt
2-1/4 teaspoons baking soda
2-1/4 teaspoons ground ginger
1-1/2 teaspoons ground cloves
1-1/2 teaspoons ground cinnamon

In a large mixing bowl, cream together butter, shortening and sugar until light-colored and fluffy. Beat in molasses and eggs; set mixture aside. In another large bowl, combine flour (no need to sift), salt, baking soda, ginger, cloves and cinnamon. Blend thoroughly with wire whisk. Gradually mix flour mixture into creamed ingredients until dough is blended and smooth. Roll dough into 1-1/2-in. balls. Dip tops in granulated sugar; place 2-1/2 in. apart on greased cookie sheet. Bake at 350° for 11 minutes. *Do not overbake.* Cool on wire rack. Store in tightly covered container to maintain softness. **Yield:** About 3 dozen cookies.

PICNIC PICKUPS: Pack cut-up chunks of watermelon, rind removed, in a chilled container for a refreshing snack.

● When there won't be a grill handy, fill a large-mouth thermos with boiling water and drop in a few hot dogs. They'll heat in transit—kids think they're great!

SIX-BEAN CASSEROLE

Marsha Ransom, South Haven, Michigan

(PICTURED ON PAGE 54)

1/2 pound bulk sweet Italian sausage
1/4 pound pepperoni, sliced thin
1/2 pound smoked kielbasa, sliced
1/2 cup spicy barbecue sauce

1 can (16 ounces) pork and beans, *undrained*
1 can (16 ounces) red kidney beans, *undrained*
1 can (16 ounces) hot chili beans, *undrained*
1 can (16 ounces) white kidney beans (Canellini), drained
1 can (16 ounces) butter beans, drained
1 can (16 ounces) lima beans, drained
1 can (10-3/4 ounces) tomato soup, *undiluted*
3 ounces tomato paste
1/2 cup brown sugar *or* to taste
6 slices bacon

Form the Italian sausage into 1-in. balls. Brown in skillet; drain. Combine with remaining ingredients, except bacon, in 5-qt. casserole or in small roasting pan. Partially cook bacon in microwave or on stovetop; arrange over casserole. Bake, uncovered, at 325° for 1-1/2 hours. Serve hot or cold. **Yield:** 16 generous servings.

PICNIC POINTERS: Fill clean, plastic gallon jugs with water and freeze. They'll help keep cold foods cold, and as the water melts it can be used for drinking—or rinsing hands and faces.

● Keep a casserole hot by wrapping the dish in heavy towels. Carry it in a cardboard box.

PICNIC HERO SANDWICH

Anne Frederick, New Hartford, New York

1/3 cup bottled chili sauce
3 tablespoons mayonnaise
1/4 teaspoon Worcestershire sauce
1 pound loaf French *or* Italian bread
8 lettuce leaves
1-1/2 cups prepared coleslaw
4 roasted *or* grilled chicken breast halves, sliced thin
1 jar (11 ounces) sweet roasted red peppers *or* sliced fresh tomatoes

Combine chili sauce, mayonnaise and Worcestershire sauce in a small bowl and set aside. Using a long, serrated knife, slice bread lengthwise to form *three layers.* Spread each cut surface with chili sauce mixture. Top each layer with lettuce, coleslaw, sliced chicken and peppers/tomatoes. Reassemble the loaf and cut into thick slices for serving. **Yield:** 6 large servings.

ADREANA'S GREEK PASTA SALAD

Lee Souleles, Northridge, California

(PICTURED ON PAGE 56)

1 pound rotini noodles
1 pound boneless chicken breasts
3 stalks celery, chopped
1 sweet red pepper, chopped
1 can (2-1/4 ounces) sliced black olives
1 package (4 ounces) Feta cheese, drained and crumbled
3 green onions, finely sliced
1 bottle (16 ounces) Italian dressing

Cook noodles according to package directions. Cook chicken breasts in water to cover with 1 bay leaf, 30 minutes or until juices run clear. Cool; remove skin. Cut chicken in bite-size pieces. Combine noodles, chicken, celery, pepper, olives, cheese, onions and salad dressing. Serve warm or cold. **Yield:** 16 servings.

COMPANY POTATOES

Mrs. James Grisdale, Mt. Pleasant, Michigan

(PICTURED ON PAGE 56)

1/2 cup chopped onions
1/4 cup butter
1 can (10-3/4 ounces) cream of chicken soup, undiluted
2 pounds frozen hash brown potatoes
1 pint dairy sour cream
TOPPING:
2 cups shredded cheddar cheese
1 cup corn flake crumbs

Saute onions in butter until transparent. Add soup, potatoes and sour cream. Spoon into a greased 13-in. x 9-in. x 2-in. baking pan. Combine cheese and corn flakes; spread over top. Bake at 350° for 45 minutes. **Yield:** 12 servings.

DEBBIE'S DEVILED EGGS

Debbie Lampert, Milton, Wisconsin

(PICTURED ON PAGE 56)

6 large eggs
1/16 teaspoon ground white pepper
1-1/2 teaspoons prepared Dijon mustard

1/4 cup creamy salad dressing
1 teaspoon dill pickle juice, optional (reduce salad dressing amount if used)
Paprika *or* dill weed

Before cooking eggs, use a tack to pierce a hole in the broad end of the egg —this centers the yolk. Cook eggs by placing, single layer, in heavy saucepan. Add cold water to cover eggs by at least 1 inch. Bring to boil; cover, shut off heat and let stand on burner for 20 minutes. Pour off hot water; replace with cold. Change water several times until eggs are cold. Push eggs against each other in water to crack shells (loosens the membrane and allows easy peeling). Peel eggs under running water; drain and slice in half, lengthwise, beginning at narrow end. Remove yolks; mash yolks with fork. Combine yolk with pepper, mustard, dressing and pickle juice, if desired. Fill cavities using pastry tube. Nest on a bed of alfalfa sprouts; sprinkle with paprika or dill weed or decorate with strip of pimiento. **Yield:** 12 deviled egg halves.

SPICED CHICKEN WINGS

Marion Stanley, Gilroy, California

(PICTURED ON PAGE 56)

12 whole chicken wings
SAUCE:
3/4 cup soy sauce
1 clove garlic, pressed
1/2 teaspoon dark roasted sesame oil
1/2 teaspoon powdered ginger
Pinch of Chinese 5-Spice powder

Remove tips from chicken wings. Cut each wing in half at joint; set aside. Combine sauce ingredients in bowl or heavy-duty plastic bag; add wing pieces and marinate, refrigerated, 1 hour or more. Remove wing pieces from sauce and place, thick-skin side down, in a lightly greased shallow baking pan. Pour sauce over wings. Bake at 375° for 20 minutes. Remove from oven and pour off juices and sauce, reserving liquid. Turn wings. Return to oven; bake 20 minutes more until browned. Serve hot or cold. (Reserved liquid can be heated and used as a dipping sauce.) **Yield:** 4-6 servings.

BIBB LETTUCE SALAD

Marcella Swigert, Monroe City, Missouri

(PICTURED ON PAGE 57)

1 head Bibb lettuce
1 head iceberg lettuce
1 bunch fresh spinach
1 bunch escarole
1 bunch endive
1 head Boston lettuce
DRESSING:
1 cup corn oil
6 tablespoons sugar
1 teaspoon dry mustard
1-4 tablespoons onion, chopped
1/2 cup apple cider vinegar
1 teaspoon celery seed
GARNISHES:
3 ounces blue cheese, crumbled
8 ounces bacon, fried and crumbled

Rinse greens; drain well. Tear greens into bite-size pieces; mix thoroughly in large salad bowl. Chill. Combine dressing ingredients in blender; blend well. Sprinkle garnishes over greens; pour dressing over all and toss gently. **Yield:** 20 servings.

DELAWARE CHICKEN DIVAN

Joan Rae Mills, Greenwood, Delaware

(PICTURED ON PAGE 57)

2 packages (10 ounces *each*) frozen broccoli *or* 1-1/2 pounds fresh broccoli, washed, cut in spears and lightly steamed
1-1/2 cups cooked chicken white meat, cut in bite-size pieces
SAUCE:
1 can (10-3/4 ounces) cream of chicken soup, *undiluted*
1/2 cup mayonnaise
2 tablespoons fresh lemon juice
2 tablespoons sherry *or* chicken broth
1/4 cup Parmesan cheese

Arrange broccoli spears on bottom of 1-1/2-qt. buttered casserole; sprinkle chicken pieces over broccoli. Combine sauce ingredients; spoon over top of broccoli/chicken. Bake uncovered at 350° for 30 minutes. **Yield:** 4 servings.

ZESTY CARROTS
James McMonagle, Bethel Park, Pennsylvania

(PICTURED ON PAGE 57)

**1-1/2 pounds carrots, washed
and peeled
1/4 cup water, reserved from
cooking carrots
2 tablespoons grated onion
and juice
1 tablespoon prepared
horseradish
1/2 cup mayonnaise
1/4 cup grated cheddar cheese
1/2 teaspoon salt
1/4 teaspoon pepper**
TOPPING:
**1 cup fresh bread crumbs
1/4 cup butter, melted
1 teaspoon paprika**

Slice carrots 1/4 in. thick; cook in small amount of water for 5 minutes. Drain; reserve 1/4 cup of water for sauce. Combine water, onion/juice, horseradish, mayonnaise, cheese, salt and pepper. Add carrots and spoon into buttered 2-qt. casserole. Combine topping ingredients; sprinkle over carrot mixture. Bake at 350° for 20 minutes. **Yield:** 8 servings.

CHEESEBURGER ONION PIE
Sharon Jakovac, Salmon, Idaho

(PICTURED ON PAGE 57)

**1 tablespoon vegetable oil
1 pound mild white onions,
sliced and quartered to make
3 cups
1 pound ground beef
1/3 cup catsup
2 teaspoons prepared mustard
1/4 teaspoon salt
1/8 teaspoon ground pepper
2 cans (8 ounces each)
refrigerated crescent dinner
rolls
1 cup shredded cheddar cheese
2 eggs, beaten**
GLAZE:
**1 egg yolk, beaten
1 tablespoon water**

Heat oil in skillet over medium heat. Add onions; cook, covered, for 10 minutes, stirring occasionally. Remove onions; set aside. Brown ground beef; remove from heat and drain off fat. Stir in catsup, mustard, salt and pepper; set aside. On floured surface, unroll dough from 1 can of rolls. Press together perforations and roll dough to 12-in. square. Place dough in a 9-in. quiche dish, tart pan or pie plate; trim to 1 in. beyond edge of dish. Spoon meat mixture into dish. Sprinkle with cheese; top with onions. Pour two beaten eggs over onion layer. Unroll remaining roll dough; press together perforations and roll out to an 11-in. square. Place on top of onion layer; trim and pinch together with bottom dough layer. Combine glaze ingredients; brush over surface. Bake at 350° for 40 minutes or until browned. Let stand 10 minutes before serving. Serve with chili sauce, if desired. **Yield:** 8 servings.

SOUR CREAM PEAR PIE
Susan Mason, Twin Falls, Idaho

(PICTURED ON PAGE 58)

**2 cups peeled, diced ripe pears
1/2 cup sugar
1 egg, beaten
1 tablespoon flour
1 cup dairy sour cream
1 teaspoon vanilla**
Dash salt
1 *unbaked* 9-inch pastry shell
CRUMB TOPPING:
**1/2 cup sugar
1/3 cup flour
1/4 cup butter, softened**

Combine pears, sugar, egg, flour, sour cream, vanilla and salt; blend gently. Spoon into unbaked pie shell. Bake at 350° for 25 minutes. Combine all of the topping ingredients till well-mixed. Sprinkle on top of pie; return to oven for 30 minutes more. **Yield:** 8 servings.

CHOCOLATE FUDGE CAKE
Pat Schaffer, Bark River, Michigan

(PICTURED ON PAGE 58)

**1/2 cup butter
1-1/2 cups sugar
2 large eggs
1 teaspoon vanilla
1/2 cup plus 1 tablespoon hot
water
2/3 cup unsweetened cocoa
1-3/4 cups unsifted all-purpose flour
1 teaspoon baking soda
1 teaspoon baking powder
1/2 teaspoon salt
1 cup sour milk (1 tablespoon
white vinegar plus milk to
1 cup)**

CHOCOLATE CREAM FROSTING:
**3 squares (3 ounces)
unsweetened chocolate
1/4 cup butter
2 cups confectioners' sugar
1/2 cup dairy sour cream
2 teaspoons vanilla**

To make cake, combine softened butter and sugar until fluffy. Add eggs, one at a time, beating well after each addition. Mix in vanilla. Stir hot water into cocoa to form a smooth paste; add gradually to creamed mixture. Set aside. Combine flour, baking soda, powder and salt; add to creamed mixture alternately with sour milk. Pour batter into two greased-and-floured 9-in. layer pans. Bake at 350° for 30-35 minutes or until wooden pick inserted in center comes out clean. Cool cake 10 minutes in pans; remove from pans to wire racks to complete cooling. Chill before frosting. To make frosting, combine chocolate and butter in small saucepan and melt over low heat, stirring to blend. Pour chocolate/butter mixture into small mixing bowl. Add remaining ingredients; beat until smooth and creamy. **Yield:** 16 servings.

CHICKEN CASSEROLE
Bonnie Ziegler, Rincon, Georgia

**2 cups cooked chopped
chicken
1/2 cup chopped pecans
2 teaspoons instant minced
onion
2 cups sliced celery
1 cup mayonnaise
2 teaspoons lemon juice
1 cup potato chips, broken in
small pieces
1/2 cup mild grated cheddar
cheese**

Mix all ingredients together *except cheese and chips*. Put into a 1-1/2-quart casserole pan or dish Mix chips and cheese. Sprinkle on top. Bake, uncovered, at 375° about 30 minutes or until heated through. **Yield:** 6 servings.

READY-TO-GO GEAR: Keep needed picnic supplies in a separate basket or box and you'll never be caught without the salt again!

Pack silverware, serving spoons, plates, cups, a sharp knife, tablecloth, can opener, salt, pepper and a roll of paper towels and you'll be sure of complete supplies on a moment's notice.

MAIN DISH TUNA SALAD

Twyla Richett, North Hampton, New Hampshire

7 ounces pasta shells *or* spirals
1 can (7 ounces) chunk tuna, drained
1/2 cup chopped celery
1/2 cup chopped carrots
1/2 cup finely chopped green onions
1/2 cup chopped sweet pickle
3 hard-cooked eggs, chopped

DRESSING:
1/2 cup mayonnaise
1 to 2 tablespoons sweet pickle juice (to taste)
1 tablespoon prepared mustard
1/2 teaspoon salt
Freshly ground pepper

Cook pasta according to package directions. Drain; cool. Combine tuna, celery, carrots, green onions, pickle and eggs in a large bowl; add pasta. Blend dressing ingredients. Pour over all; stir to mix. Chill thoroughly. Must be kept chilled. **Yield:** 6-8 servings.

RED, WHITE AND BLUE SALAD

Lanette Wiedner Larson, Washington, D.C.

(PICTURED ON PAGE 58)

1 package (3 ounces) strawberry gelatin dessert
1 envelope unflavored gelatin
1 cup sugar
1 cup whipping cream
2 cups dairy sour cream
1 teaspoon vanilla
1 package (3 ounces) raspberry *or* black cherry gelatin dessert
1 can (15 ounces) canned blueberries, packed in syrup *or* water

Note: This salad takes time to prepare, since each layer must set until firm before the next layer is added. Dissolve 1 package of strawberry gelatin dessert in 2 cups boiling water; pour into 3-qt. glass bowl. Refrigerate until firmly set. Dissolve 1 envelope of unflavored gelatin in 1/2 cup cold water; set aside. Over low heat, carefully dissolve sugar in whipping cream; heat, stirring constantly, until mixture *nearly* boils. Remove from heat; add unflavored gelatin mixture. Cool. Blend in sour cream and vanilla; pour over first layer. Re-

frigerate until firm. Dissolve 1 package of raspberry/black cherry gelatin dessert in 1 cup boiling water; cool. Add 1 can blueberries and juice. Pour over second layer; refrigerate until firm. Refrigerate any leftovers. **Yield:** 10 servings.

BUTTERMILK COCONUT PIE

Marie Brown, Carthage, Mississippi

(PICTURED ON PAGE 58)

1-1/4 cups sugar
2 tablespoons all-purpose flour (*not* self-rising)
1/2 cup butter, melted
3 eggs, beaten
1/2 cup cultured buttermilk
1 teaspoon vanilla extract
1 can (3-1/2 ounces) flaked coconut, *divided*
1 *unbaked* 9-inch pastry shell

Combine the sugar and flour in a large bowl. Add melted butter, eggs, buttermilk, vanilla and two-thirds of the coconut. Mix well. Pour mixture into shell. Sprinkle with remaining coconut. Bake at 325° for 1 hour and 5 minutes or until set. **Yield:** 8 servings.

ARTICHOKE GREEN CHILI BAKE

Sylvia Teague, Eureka Springs, Arkansas

3 jars (6 ounces *each*) marinated artichokes
1 medium onion, chopped, about 1/2 cup
1 clove garlic, minced
10 eggs, beaten
1/2 cup fine breadcrumbs
4 cups grated Monterey Jack cheese
1/2 teaspoon salt
1/2 teaspoon dried leaf basil
1/2 teaspoon dried leaf oregano
1/4 teaspoon pepper
1 can (4 ounces) chopped green chilies

Drain artichokes, reserving 2 tablespoons marinade. Coarsely chop artichokes; set aside. Saute onion and garlic in reserved marinade. Mix with eggs, breadcrumbs, cheese, salt, basil, oregano, pepper and chilies. Pour into two 8-inch square baking dishes. Bake at 325° for 35-40 minutes or until set. Cut into squares to serve as appetizers. **Yield:** About 50 appetizer squares.

PLATZ

(Traditional Mennonite Fruit Dessert)
Edith Quapp, Yarrow, British Columbia

CAKE:
2 cups all-purpose flour
2 teaspoons baking powder
1 cup sugar
1/8 teaspoon salt
1/2 cup butter
1 cup milk
2 eggs, beaten
2 teaspoons vanilla

FRUIT LAYER:
Fresh or frozen unsweetened fruit of choice—apples, cherries, blueberries, plums, blackberries, apricots, peaches or nectarines

TOPPING:
1/4 cup melted butter
3/4 cup all-purpose flour
3/4 cup sugar

Blend flour, baking powder, sugar, salt and butter in a large bowl. Stir in milk, beaten eggs and vanilla. Spread batter on well-greased 17-in. x 11-1/2-in. x 1-in. baking sheet or jelly roll pan. Cover with fruit of choice. Combine topping ingredients and mix by hand until crumbly; sprinkle over fruit. Bake at 375° for 30-35 minutes. **Yield:** 40 squares (2 inches each).

HARVEST POTATO CASSEROLE

Cheryl Farmon, Lawrence, Nebraska

6 cups frozen shredded hash brown potatoes, thawed
1/3 cup chopped onion
2 cups dairy sour cream
1/2 teaspoon salt
1/4 teaspoon ground pepper
1 pound little smoked sausage links
1 cup shredded cheddar cheese

Combine all ingredients except sausage and cheese. Put in 13-in. x 9-in. x 2-in. baking pan. Arrange sausage links on top of potato mixture. Cover; bake at 350° for 35 minutes or until bubbly. Sprinkle the shredded cheese over top; bake, uncovered, 5 minutes more. **Yield:** 6 servings.

SQUASH CASSEROLE

Bonnie Ziegler, Rincon, Georgia

3 to 4 cups coarsely chopped
summer squash, cooked
1 cup dairy sour cream
1 onion, chopped
1 can (10-3/4 ounces) cream of
chicken soup
1 carrot, grated
6 saltine crackers, crushed
1/2 cup mild grated cheddar
cheese
Salt to taste
Ground pepper to taste

Butter a 2-quart square casserole dish. Combine *all* ingredients *except cheese* and pour into dish. Bake, covered at 375° about 30 minutes or until heated through. Uncover and add cheese the last 5 minutes. **Yield:** 6-8 servings.

MANICOTTI

Sylvia Teague, Eureka Springs, Arkansas

DOUGH:
1-1/4 cups whole wheat flour
2 eggs
FILLING:
1 container (15 ounces) ricotta
cheese
1/2 teaspoon salt
1/4 teaspoon ground pepper
1 teaspoon dried leaf basil
1/4 cup grated Parmesan cheese
2 cups grated mozzarella
cheese, *divided*
2 eggs
SAUCE:
1 quart fresh *or* canned
tomatoes
2 tablespoons vegetable oil
1 chopped onion
1 green pepper, diced
1 sweet red pepper, diced
2 cloves garlic
1 can (6 ounces) tomato paste
1/4 pound fresh mushrooms,
chopped
1/4 cup dry red wine, optional
1/2 to 2 teaspoons salt
1/4 teaspoon pepper
2 teaspoons dried leaf basil
1 teaspoon dried leaf oregano
1/2 teaspoon dried rosemary

Mix dough well; knead on floured board until smooth. Form into ball, cover, let stand at least 1 hour. While dough rests, make sauce by pureeing tomatoes in blender; set aside. Saute in oil, onion, peppers and garlic. Add pureed tomatoes and remaining sauce ingredi-

ents; simmer 30 minutes or more. Divide dough in one-half. Roll *each half* into a 16-in. x 10-in. rectangle. Cut each rectangle into six 5-in. x 4-in. rectangles. Set aside. Combine filling ingredients (*reserving 1 cup cheese*); beat well together. Place one-twelfth of filling on one long edge of each rectangle; roll up. Pour one-half of sauce on bottom of 13-in. x 9-in. x 2-in. baking dish. Place filled manicotti, seam side down, in sauce. Pour remaining sauce over. Sprinkle with reserved cheese and freshly chopped parsley, if desired. Cover with foil; bake at 350° for 30-45 minutes. **Yield:** 6 servings.

CREAM OF ASPARAGUS SOUP

Linda Garringer, Marion, Indiana

4 tablespoons butter, *divided*
2 tablespoons all-purpose flour
1 bunch (10 ounces) fresh
asparagus*
1 small onion, *finely chopped*
1 quart chicken stock *or* broth
1/2 cup heavy cream, *warmed*
Salt
Pepper

*You may substitute about 2 cups of broccoli or cauliflower for asparagus. Melt 2 tablespoons butter in small saucepan; stir in flour. Cook 3 minutes over low heat, stirring constantly. Cool. Wash and cut asparagus into 1/2-inch pieces, reserving 1/4 cup tips for garnish. Saute onion in remaining 2 tablespoons butter in large saucepan until tender. Stir in asparagus; cover. Cook for 3 minutes. Stir in stock/broth; heat to simmering. Stir a small amount of asparagus/stock mixture into butter/flour mixture until smooth; return blended mixture to saucepan, stirring until smooth. Simmer, covered, until asparagus is tender, about 20 minutes. Remove from heat; cool slightly. Puree in small amounts in container of electric blender; return to saucepan. Blend cream into soup. Taste; add salt and pepper, if needed. Steam asparagus tips in microwave or on stove until tender/crisp. Spoon soup into individual bowls; garnish with tips. **Yield:** 6 servings.

BETTER BURGERS: For a juicier hamburger, add cold water to the beef before grilling—1/2 cup for each pound of meat.

NANCY'S PEPPERMINT COOKIES

Nancy Schuman, Franklin, Indiana

1 cup margarine
1 cup brown sugar
1 egg
2 cups sifted all-purpose flour
1 teaspoon baking soda
1/2 teaspoon salt
2 cups quick-cooking oats
1/2 cup crushed peppermint
candy
GLAZE:
1-1/2 cups sifted confectioner's
sugar
3 tablespoons milk
3 tablespoons crushed
peppermint candy

Beat margarine and brown sugar in mixing bowl until light and fluffy. Blend in egg. Set aside. Sift together flour, soda and salt. Add dry ingredients to creamed mixture; mix well. Stir in quick oats and peppermint; mixing well. Roll in 1-inch balls and place 2 inches apart on ungreased cookie sheet. Bake for 10-12 minutes. Cool 1 minute; remove from cookie sheet. Cool completely. Combine sugar and milk for glaze; mix well. Drizzle glaze over cooled cookies; sprinkle with crushed peppermint candy. **Yield:** About 4 dozen.

PORK TENDERLOIN WITH PARMESAN CRUST

The Inn at Cedar Falls
Logan, Ohio

1 whole pork tenderloin, 15 ounces
1/2 cup flour
1/2 teaspoon salt
1/2 teaspoon pepper
1/2 cup butter, *divided*
1 shallot
1/2 cup dry white wine
1/4 cup shredded Parmesan cheese
1/4 cup fine bread crumbs

Preheat oven to 375°. Slice tenderloin in 1/4 inch slices; pound thin between sheets of waxed paper. Dip into flour/salt/pepper mixture and saute very quickly in 2 tablespoons of butter. Place in single layer in 11-in. x 9-in. x 2-in. baking dish. Dice shallot, saute; add white wine and deglaze pan. Add to baking dish. Mix Parmesan cheese, bread crumbs and 1/4 cup butter in food processor. Make a log of the mixture, slice and press one slice on top of each slice of pork. Bake for 15-20 minutes. **Yield:** 4 servings.

COUNTRY INNS

Jordan Hollow Farm Inn

Route 2, Box 375, Stanley, Virginia 22851

Phone: 1-703/778-2209 or 703/778-2285

Directions: From Luray, Virginia, take Hwy. 340 south, left on Rte. 624, left on Rte. 689, right on Rte. 626.

Innkeepers: Marley and Jetze Beers.

Schedule: Open year-round.

Accommodations and Rates: 16 rooms with private baths, $75 double occupancy; extra person $10, children 16 and under in same room—free. Meals not included in room rates (dinners range from $7.25 to $16.95, with children's portions $5.50 to $6.50). Horseback trail rides and lessons available at additional cost. Meeting facilities for up to 32 people. Wheelchair access: possible.

"Country cosmopolitan" are the words which best describe the menu at Jordan Hollow Farm Inn. All the food served at this working Virginia horse farm is absolutely fresh and cooked to order. They feature whatever vegetables are in season—most of which are grown right at the farm. A variety of fresh herbs add zest to dishes.

Innkeeper Marley does much of the cooking herself, and the fare ranges from Ribeye Steaks cooked in the seasonings she became fond of while in the Peace Corps in North Africa to an Apple Crisp recipe from her mother.

A typical dinner may start with warm cracked-wheat bread, served with a cup of beef bouillon laced with lemon. That's followed by a garden salad, and Rainbow Trout Almondine, sauteed in herbs and lemon butter.

The ribeye recipe features steaks seasoned with cumin, garlic, and soy sauce, topped with a fresh mushroom sauce. (If you like spicier food, increase the amount of cumin slightly.) These savory steaks are a favorite of guests at the Jordan Hollow Farm Inn.

MARLEY'S RIBEYE STEAK

- 6 ribeye steaks
- 3 tablespoons soy sauce
- 1 tablespoon minced garlic
- 1 teaspoon ground cumin (or to taste)
- 1/8 teaspoon freshly ground pepper
- 1/4 cup butter

MUSHROOM SAUCE:
- 1 pound fresh mushrooms, sliced
- 1/4 cup butter
- 2 tablespoons white wine
- 1/8 teaspoon each cumin, powdered garlic, pepper and salt

Season steaks with soy sauce, garlic, cumin and pepper; set aside. Saute mushrooms in 1/4 cup butter; add wine and sprinkle with seasonings. Saute seasoned steaks in 1/4 cup butter (or grill) to desired doneness; top with sauce. **Yield:** 6 servings.

RAINBOW TROUT ALMONDINE

- 2 fresh rainbow trout
- 2 tablespoons soy sauce *or* light soy sauce
- 1/2 teaspoon ground or finely chopped rosemary
- 3/4 teaspoon ground or finely chopped garlic
- 1/4 cup cornmeal
- 1/2 cup flour
- 1/4 cup Parmesan cheese
- 1/2 cup butter, *divided*
- 2 tablespoons lemon juice (or to taste)

Garnish—toasted almonds, fresh dill, sliced lemon

Rinse trout thoroughly, season inside by rubbing with soy sauce. Lightly sprinkle with rosemary and garlic. Close fish and dip in a mixture of cornmeal, flour and Parmesan cheese. Open fish, saute skin side down in 1/4 cup butter until brown. Lay fish (still open) in pan and bake in 400° oven for a few minutes until the meat flakes. Remove from oven, close and put on warmed plate. Pour out pan drippings, add remaining butter and lemon juice to taste, scraping up pan drippings. Pour over trout, garnish with toasted almonds, fresh dill and sliced lemon. **Yield:** 2 servings.

MOTHER'S APPLE CRISP

- 6 cups Macintosh or Granny Smith apples, peeled, cored and sliced, *divided*
- 1/3 cup orange juice
- 1/2 teaspoon vanilla
- 2 tablespoons rum *or* apple schnapps (optional)
- 3/4 cup brown sugar
- 1/2 cup white sugar
- 3/4 cup flour
- 1 teaspoon cinnamon
- 1/2 cup regular oatmeal
- 1/4 cup chopped pecans
- 3/4 cup (1-1/2 sticks) butter, melted

Preheat oven to 325°. Butter a glass baking dish (7-1/2-in. x 11-1/2-in.) and place half the sliced apples in the dish. Mix juice, vanilla and rum or schnapps; pour half the mixture over apples. Mix dry ingredients and sprinkle half the mixture over the apples. Add remaining apples, sprinkle with remaining liquids and spread remaining dry ingredients. Drizzle melted butter on top. Bake in pre-heated oven for 90 minutes. Serve with freshly made whipped cream or vanilla ice cream. **Yield:** 8 servings.

For another variation on herb vinegars, see recipe on page 17.

HERB VINEGARS:

3-1/2 cups white vinegar or *wine vinegar*
Seasonings/herbs of choice

Scald a 1-quart bottle with a tight-fitting top; let dry completely. Place desired herb/seasonings in bottle. Heat vinegar in medium saucepan just to boiling. Let cool slightly; pour into bottle. Let cool. Seal tightly. Let stand in dark place at room temperature for 2-3 weeks, shaking occasionally. Strain and rebottle with sprigs of fresh herbs.

HERBED WHITE VINEGAR

2 sprigs parsley
2 sprigs fresh dill
1 medium red onion, sliced
8 whole peppercorns
2 celery stalks with leaves

GARLIC RED WINE VINEGAR

6 cloves garlic, peeled
2 sprigs parsley
1 bay leaf
8 whole peppercorns
1/2 teaspoon crushed red pepper flakes

BEST COOK

Growing boys are known for their appetites. But not many boys are known for their culinary abilities —at least to where they can out-cook the competition in a national contest!

We know one who can. He's 17-year-old Bill Hill of tiny Trout Creek, Montana, who was nominated as "Best Cook in the Country" by Jay Simons of nearby Noxon.

"I've known Bill a long time, and I'm very proud of his accomplishments," Jay wrote. "His 'Rancher's Barbecued Beef Ribs' recently won second prize in a contest in New York City...and that's not the first contest he's won, either! His goal is to be a professional chef, and he's been saving his prize money to pay for cooking school after he graduated from high school."

Bill's Home Economics teacher, Sandra Davis, has encouraged his enthusiasm for cooking.

"When I got into seventh grade, Miss Davis taught me the proper use of kitchen utensils and ways to cut up different vegetables for various dishes," Bill recalls. "I'll never forget my first cooking project. She told me 'Muffins should never have peaks and tunnels.'"

Bill learned his lesson well, and today, his muffins are matchless! "I also like baking pastries, especially cream puffs and chocolate eclairs. Cooking and baking are relaxing for me...and exciting, too, when I win contests. Of course, I love to eat!"

LASAGNA (MICROWAVE)

- 1 **pound lean ground beef** *or* **Italian sausage**
- 1 **can (14-1/2 ounces) tomatoes, undrained & chopped**
- 1 **can (6 ounces) tomato paste**
- 1-1/2 **teaspoons salt**
- 1-1/2 **teaspoons dried basil leaves, crushed**
- 1/2 **teaspoon dried oregano leaves, crushed**
- 1/8 **teaspoon garlic powder**
- 1/2 **cup water**
- 2 **cups cottage cheese**
- 1/4 **cup grated Parmesan cheese**
- 1 **egg**
- 1 **tablespoon dried parsley flakes**
- 8 *uncooked* **lasagna noodles**
- 2 **cups shredded mozzarella cheese**
- 2 **tablespoons grated Parmesan cheese**

Place a plastic colander in quart glass measure or microwave safe bowl. Crumble meat into colander. Microwave (MW) on HIGH for 3 minutes. Stir with fork to break meat in small pieces. MW 1-1/2 to 3 minutes on HIGH until meat is cooked. Stir with fork; pour grease off meat. Place meat in 2-quart microwave-safe dish. Stir in tomatoes, tomato paste, salt, basil, oregano, garlic powder and water. Cover with lid or plastic; MW on HIGH for 3 minutes; stir. Recover; MW 2 minutes on HIGH until mixture boils. Set aside. In medium sized mixing bowl, combine cottage cheese, 1/4 cup Parmesan cheese, egg and parsley. Mix well. Pour 1-1/2 cups of tomato sauce evenly into 12-in. x 8-in. x 3-in. baking dish. Place four uncooked noodles evenly over sauce (may overlap slightly). Top with one-half of cottage cheese mixture, spreading evenly. Sprinkle with one-half of mozzarella cheese. Spoon 1 cup of sauce evenly over cheese. Place remaining noodles over sauce. Top with layers of remaining cottage cheese mixture, mozzarella cheese and tomato sauce. Cover with vented plastic wrap. MW on HIGH for 15 minutes, rotating dish 1/2 turn after 7 minutes. MW on MEDIUM for 15-20 minutes more until noodles are tender. Carefully remove plastic wrap (away from you) to avoid steam burns. Sprinkle lasagna with 2 tablespoons Parmesan cheese. MW on HIGH, uncovered, for 1-1/2 minutes or until cheese is melted. Let stand about 10 minutes before cutting into squares. **Yield:** 8 servings.

BILL'S MONTANA SWISS STEAK

- 1-1/2 **pounds round steak**
- 3 **tablespoons all-purpose flour**
- 1 **teaspoon salt**
- 1/4 **teaspoon ground pepper**
- 1/2 **teaspoon chili powder**
- 2 **tablespoons vegetable shortening**
- 1 **can (16 ounces) tomatoes, chopped**
- 1 **small onion, sliced**
- 1 **stalk celery, sliced**
- 1 **medium carrot, thinly sliced**
- 1/2 **to 1 teaspoon Worcestershire sauce**
- 1 **green pepper, sliced**
- **Hot cooked rice** *or* **noodles**

Cut meat into 6 serving-size pieces. Combine flour, salt, pepper and chili powder; pound 2 tablespoons of mixture into meat. Brown meat on both sides in 10-inch skillet in hot shortening. Drain excess fat. Add undrained tomatoes, onion, celery, carrot, Worcestershire sauce and pepper. Cover; simmer for 1 hour and 15 minutes. Remove meat; place on a warm serving plate. Skim excess fat off sauce. Combine 1/4 cup water with remaining flour mixture, stirring into tomato sauce. Cook and stir for 2 more minutes. Pass with meat. Serve with hot cooked rice or noodles. **Yield:** 6 servings.

CHUCK WAGON BEANS

- 2 **cans (1 pound** *each***) pork & beans**
- 1/2 **cup catsup**
- 1/4 **cup brown sugar**
- 1 **teaspoon Dijon mustard**
- 1/3 **cup bottled steak sauce**
- 8 **slices Canadian bacon**
- 1/3 **cup chopped onion**
- **Grated cheese**
- **Tortilla chips**

In 2-quart saucepan, combine beans, catsup, sugar, mustard, steak sauce and bacon. Stir until mixture boils. Reduce heat; simmer for 20 minutes. To serve, top with chopped onions and grated cheese. Garnish with tortilla chips. **Yield:** 6-8 servings.

Fall flavors fill our hearty harvest table in recipes for foods from fields, forest and garden.

For a delicious change of taste, try game dishes such as Pheasant with Creamy Yogurt Sauce or Rabbit Dijon. (Or use poultry in either recipe, if you prefer.)

As an accompaniment, consider Potato Bread, Oven Fried Potatoes or Wild Rice Soup. And savor the season's abundant vegetables in flavorful new ways with Herb Scalloped Tomatoes and crisp/tender Smothered Green Cabbage. Add color and tart taste to the table with Cranberry Plus Relish.

Enjoy the abundance of the season with any (or all) of these fine fall dishes!

FALL FAVORITES: Clockwise on our harvest table from lower left—**Pheasant with Creamy Yogurt Sauce,** Pat Breidenbach, Mitchell, South Dakota (Pg. 75); **Cranberry Plus Relish,** Marion Reader, Medford, New Jersey (Pg. 75); **Herb Scalloped Tomatoes,** Lorrie Martin, Phoenix, Arizona (Pg. 75); **Potato Bread,** Lynn Clarke, Bellevue, Idaho (Pg. 75); **Wild Rice Soup,** Elmelda Johnson, East Grand Forks, Minnesota (Pg. 76); **Smothered Green Cabbage,** Joan Knox, Chicago, Illinois (Pg. 76); **Oven Fried Potatoes,** Mary Armold, Long Prairie, Minnesota (Pg. 76); **Rabbit Dijon,** Kathryn Wolter, Sturgeon Bay, Wisconsin (Pg. 75).

Seasonal desserts make a delicious finish to color-filled days. Taste the flavors of fall in creamy, spicy Pumpkin Cake Roll or extra-rich Southern Pecan Cheesecake...or pucker up to tart/sweet Cranberry Streusel Pie or warm Apple Fritters. These autumn delights capture the savory, spicy tastes of the waning year. Enjoy!

SWEET HARVEST: Clockwise from the lower left—**Apple Fritters,** Ruby Nelson, Mountain Home, Arkansas (Pg. 77); **Pumpkin Cake Roll,** Sally Weaver, New Baden, Illinois (Pg. 76); **Southern Pecan Cheesecake,** Captain Katherine Brown, Minot AFB, North Dakota (Pg. 76); **Cranberry Streusel Pie,** Mary Ellen Kiesner, Menomonee Falls, Wisconsin (Pg. 76).

Pewter from the Red Fox, Mequon, Wisconsin

Antiques courtesy of the "Oh, To Be In England" Shop, Milwaukee, Wisconsin

MEALS IN MINUTES

BUSY FAMILIES with varied schedules can make supper planning difficult. For your short-on-notice suppers, stock your pantry with convenient, easy-to-prepare foods. One staple is versatile, tasty canned salmon—especially tasty in this quick Salmon Burger recipe.

Start your speedy supper by preparing Honey-Celery Seed Dressing in the blender, and refrigerating it until mealtime. This dressing is delicious over a variety of greens—cabbage, lettuce or even spinach.

While you pan-fry or oven-broil the Salmon Burgers, cut the salad ingredients and slice and toast whole-wheat buns. You might want to make a stovetop macaroni and cheese or other convenience side dish, but potato chips will do in a pinch.

For a flavorful finish to a fast feast, serve up cups of lemon-flavored frozen yogurt, rimmed by small ginger snaps.

BROILED SALMON BURGERS

- 2 cups fine soft bread crumbs
- 2 large egg whites
- 1/4 cup chili sauce
- 1 tablespoon fresh lemon juice
- 1/4 cup minced green onions
- 1/2 cup finely grated cheddar cheese
- 1/8 teaspoon ground black pepper
- 1 can (15-1/2 ounces) salmon, skinned, boned and drained
- 1 tablespoon butter, melted

Combine crumbs, egg whites, chili sauce, lemon juice, onions, cheese and pepper in medium-sized bowl and mix well. Flake salmon into bowl and blend gently. Form salmon mixture into five patties. Melt butter in non-stick skillet; pan-fry the patties over medium-low heat about 5 minutes on each side or until golden brown (Patties may also be brushed with melted butter and oven-broiled, 3-4 in. from heat.) Serve on toasted whole wheat buns with extra chili sauce. **Yield:** 5 burgers.

CONFETTI COLESLAW

- 4 cups shredded green cabbage
- 1/2 cup diced red pepper
- 1/2 cup diced green pepper

HONEY-CELERY SEED DRESSING:

- 3 tablespoons honey
- 1 teaspoon dry mustard
- 1 teaspoon paprika
- 1/4 teaspoon salt
- 1 tablespoon lemon juice
- 1/4 cup vinegar
- 1/8 teaspoon minced dried onion
- 1 cup vegetable oil
- 1 teaspoon celery seed

Combine cabbage and peppers in a glass bowl; refrigerate, covered. Next, combine honey, mustard, paprika, salt, lemon juice, vinegar and onion in blender. Slowly add oil through top opening, continuing to blend until thick. Stir in celery seeds. Cover; store in refrigerator. Before serving coleslaw, spoon on dressing and toss to coat evenly. **Yield:** 1-1/2 cups.

Here's another quick and easy vegetable recipe:

MICROWAVE VEGETABLE PLATE

Lois Wilger, Lamar, Colorado

Whole fresh mushrooms, cleaned
Summer squash, washed and diced
Cauliflower, broken into flowerettes
Broccoli, broken into flowerettes
Carrots, sliced in 1/2-inch slices
- 1 tablespoon butter
- 1 to 2 tablespoons water

Arrange vegetables on round, flat dish with mushrooms in center, squash in next circle, followed by rings of cauliflower and broccoli. Place carrots around outer edge. Microwave butter and water on HIGH until butter melts. Sprinkle plate of vegetables with mixture, cover tightly with plastic wrap. MW on HIGH for 6-8 minutes, rotating plate every 2 minutes. Salt may be added after cooking, if desired.

If you feel "good old ground beef" can't go much further in the kitchen than humdrum hamburger, hold on tight—you're in for a delicious surprise!

These different ground beef recipes are sure to cause excitement at your table—and we'll bet plenty of them will become family favorites. See for yourself how grand ground beef can be!

GROUND BEEF ROUNDUP: Clockwise from lower left—**Black Bean Chili Salad,** Carmen Gratton, New Smyrna Beach, Florida (Pg. 79); **Chili Relleno Bake,** Jan Seibert, Albion, California (Pg. 78); **Barbecued Meatballs,** Connie Johnson, Friona, Texas (Pg. 78); **Shanghai Noodles with Spicy Beef Sauce,** Ena Quiggle, Goodhue, Minnesota (Pg. 79); **Beef Casserole Italiano,** Susan Longyear, Washington, Virginia (Pg. 79); **Sunday Supper Soup,** Margaret Gage, Roseboom, New York (Pg. 79); **Tamale Pie,** Naomi Giddis, Grawn, Michigan (Pg. 80); **Taco Tartlets,** LaVonne Hartel, Williston, North Dakota (Pg. 80).

Bored with burgers? Fed up with meat loaf? Can't face another casserole? Then try these recipes. They'll restore your appetite for good old ground beef!

You'll never call Korean Beef Patties run-of-the-mill fare...not with their oriental flair! And Italian Vegetable Soup is a hearty meal-in-a-pot that's sure to become a favorite.

Colorful Mexican Lasagna features south-of-the-border flavor in an easy-to-make casserole. And who can resist a cheeseburger baked into a flaky crust in Crescent Cheeseburger Pie? Ground beef a bore? Not anymore!

GREAT GROUND BEEF: Top to bottom—**Korean Beef Patties,** Marsha Ransom, South Haven, Michigan (Pg. 81); **Italian Vegetable Soup,** Bonnie Vawter, Alton, Missouri (Pg. 81); **Mexican Lasagna,** Jeanne Bennett, Minden, Louisiana (Pg. 80); **Crescent Cheeseburger Pie,** Elinore Dumont, Drumheller, Alberta (Pg. 80).

HERB SCALLOPED TOMATOES
Lorrie Martin, Phoenix, Arizona

(PICTURED ON PAGE 68)

4 cups canned tomatoes, cut up
2-1/2 cups herb stuffing mix, *divided*
1 small onion, chopped
2 tablespoons sugar
1/2 teaspoon salt
1/2 teaspoon nutmeg
1/2 teaspoon leaf oregano, crumbled
1/4 teaspoon leaf rosemary, crumbled
1/4 teaspoon black pepper
1/4 cup butter

In a buttered 2-qt. casserole, mix together tomatoes and *2 cups* of stuffing mix. Stir in onion, sugar and seasonings. Dot with butter; sprinkle remaining stuffing mix on top. Bake at 375° for 45 minutes. **Yield:** 8 servings.

PHEASANT WITH CREAMY YOGURT SAUCE
Pat Breidenbach, Mitchell, South Dakota

(PICTURED ON PAGE 68)

1 cup fine, dry bread *or* cracker crumbs
1/4 cup grated Parmesan cheese
1 to 2 tablespoons dried minced onion
1/2 teaspoon garlic powder
1 teaspoon seasoned salt
1/4 teaspoon dried leaf oregano, crumbled
1/4 teaspoon dried leaf thyme, crumbled
Dash pepper
4 whole pheasant *or* chicken breasts, skinned, boned and halved lengthwise
1 cup mayonnaise *or* plain yogurt
1/4 cup margarine *or* butter, melted
2 teaspoons sesame seed
CREAMY YOGURT SAUCE:
1 can (10-3/4 ounces) cream of chicken soup, undiluted
1 carton (8 ounces) plain yogurt
1/2 cup chicken broth
1 teaspoon lemon juice
1/2 teaspoon Worcestershire sauce
Dash garlic powder
Dash seasoned salt

In shallow dish, combine bread/cracker crumbs, cheese, onion, garlic powder, seasoned salt, oregano, thyme and pepper. Rinse pheasant/chicken and pat dry; coat with mayonnaise/yogurt and roll in crumb mixture. Place pheasant in a lightly greased 13-in. x 9-in. x 2-in. baking dish. Drizzle margarine/butter on top. Sprinkle with sesame seed. Bake, uncovered, at 375° for 40-45 minutes until tender. Make sauce by combining all ingredients in medium saucepan and cooking over a low heat until heated through, stirring occasionally. **Yield:** 8 servings with 2-1/2 cups sauce.

CRANBERRY PLUS RELISH
Marion Reeder, Medford, New Jersey

(PICTURED ON PAGE 68)

4 cups (1 pound) fresh *or* frozen cranberries
4 oranges, peeled, sectioned and seeded
2 cups sugar (add less for tart taste)
1 apple, unpeeled, cut up
1/2 teaspoon almond flavoring
1 can (8-1/2 ounces) undrained crushed pineapple

Chop cranberries in a food processor, then add oranges and chop. Add remaining ingredients; pulse for several seconds to blend. Chill several hours before serving. **Yield:** 7-1/2 cups.

POTATO BREAD
Lynn Clarke, Bellevue, Idaho

(PICTURED ON PAGE 68)

✓ This tasty dish uses less sugar, salt and fat. Recipe includes *Diabetic Exchanges.*

1 pound potatoes, about 2 cups mashed
1-1/2 cups milk
1/3 cup butter
2 tablespoons honey
2 teaspoons salt
2 packages active dry yeast
1/2 cup warm water (110°)
2 eggs
About 8 cups all-purpose flour

Peel potatoes and boil until tender; drain and mash. Slowly stir in milk, butter, honey and salt. If necessary, heat to 110°. Meanwhile, in large bowl, mix yeast with water; let stand 5 minutes. Combine potato mixture, eggs and 3 cups flour. Gradually mix in 3-1/2 cups more flour. Turn out on floured board; knead until smooth and elastic, about 10 minutes, adding additional flour as needed. Place dough in greased bowl; turn to grease top. Cover; let rise in warm place until doubled, about 1-1/2 to 2 hours. Punch dough down; divide in thirds. Shape each portion into a smooth loaf; place in three well-greased 9-in. x 5-in. bread pans. Cover; let rise in warm place until almost double, about 30-40 minutes. Bake at 350° for 35-40 minutes or until loaves are browned and sound hollow when tapped. Turn out of pans; cool on racks. Brush with butter, if desired. **Diabetic Exchanges:** One serving equals 1 bread; also, 76 calories, 89 mg sodium, 12 mg cholesterol, 13 gm carbohydrate, 2 gm protein, 2 gm fat. **Yield:** 3 loaves (20 slices each).

RABBIT DIJON
Kathryn Wolter, Sturgeon Bay, Wisconsin

(PICTURED ON PAGE 68)

2 rabbits *or* chickens, cut in serving pieces
Salt
Pepper
1 cup flour
8 tablespoons butter, *divided*
1/4 cup brandy *or* chicken broth
1 cup chopped green onion
1/2 cup chopped parsley
1 pound fresh mushrooms, sliced
2 tablespoons Dijon mustard
1 pint sour half-and-half
Parsley for garnish

Sprinkle rabbit/chicken pieces with salt and pepper; roll in flour. Melt *4 table-spoons* butter in large skillet; brown rabbit pieces and remove to roaster. Add the brandy/broth to pan juices. Scrape browned bits from bottom and sides of skillet; pour over rabbit. Saute onion, parsley and mushrooms in remaining butter. Pour vegetable mixture over rabbit; cover and bake at 350° for 1 hour. Remove rabbit pieces to warm platter; stir mustard and half-and-half into liquid in roaster and heat. Pour sauce over rabbit on platter. (Mustard and half-and-half may also be stirred into onion, parsley, mushroom and liquid and baked as above.) **Yield:** 8-10 servings.

SMOTHERED
GREEN CABBAGE
Joan Knox, Chicago, Illinois

(PICTURED ON PAGE 69)

1/4 cup butter *or* margarine
2 tablespoons bacon drippings*
1 medium head of cabbage,
  coarsely chopped, core
  removed
1/4 teaspoon dry minced garlic
1 teaspoon caraway seeds
Salt, pepper to taste
1 can (10-3/4 ounces) cream of
  mushroom soup, undiluted

Melt butter and bacon drippings in large saucepan or Dutch oven. Add cabbage; cook and stir over medium heat until cabbage is tender/crisp, about 10 minutes. Add garlic, caraway seeds, salt and pepper. Stir in soup; heat through and serve. **Yield:** 8 servings. (*Keep bacon drippings in small blocks in freezer to preserve fresh flavor.)

OVEN-FRIED POTATOES
Mary Arnold, Long Prairie, Minnesota

(PICTURED ON PAGE 69)

4 large baking potatoes,
  unpeeled
1/4 cup vegetable oil
1 to 2 tablespoons Parmesan
  cheese
1/2 teaspoon salt
1/4 teaspoon garlic powder
1/4 teaspoon paprika
1/8 teaspoon pepper

Wash unpeeled potatoes and cut lengthwise into 4 wedges. Place skin side down in 13-in. x 9-in. x 2-in. baking dish or pan. Combine remaining ingredients; brush over potatoes. Bake at 375° for 1 hour, brushing with oil/cheese mixture at 15-minute intervals. Turn potatoes over for last 15 minutes. (These are wonderful with any roasted meat or fine as a snack.) **Yield:** 4 servings.

WILD RICE SOUP
Elmeda Johnson, East Grand Forks, Minnesota

(PICTURED ON PAGE 69)

1 cup uncooked wild rice
3 cups boiling water
2 strips smoked bacon
1/4 cup chopped onion
3/4 cup sliced celery
1/2 cup sliced carrots
1 can (14-1/2 ounces) chicken
  broth
2 cans (10-3/4 ounces *each*)
  cream of mushroom soup
2 soup cans milk
1 can (4 ounces) mushrooms,
  plus liquid
1 teaspoon seasoned salt
Pepper to taste

Combine rice and boiling water in large saucepan; simmer, covered, 50-60 minutes. Drain off excess liquid; set rice aside. Fry bacon till crisp; remove bacon and saute onion, celery and carrots in small amount of bacon fat. Combine broth, soups, milk, mushrooms, salt and pepper, reserved crumbled bacon, sauteed vegetables and wild rice. Simmer, covered, 1 hour. **Yield:** 8 servings.

CRANBERRY
STREUSEL PIE
Mary Ellen Kiesner, Menomonee Falls, Wisconsin

(PICTURED ON PAGE 70)

1/3 cup butter, softened
3/4 cup sugar
1/4 cup brown sugar, packed
1 egg
1/2 teaspoon vanilla
1 cup flour
1/2 teaspoon baking soda
1/4 teaspoon salt
2 cups fresh *or* thawed frozen
  cranberries
1/2 cup chopped walnuts
1 unbaked pie shell (9 inches)
STREUSEL TOPPING:
2 tablespoons flour
1/2 cup brown sugar, packed
1/4 teaspoon nutmeg
1/2 teaspoon cinnamon
2 tablespoons butter
1/2 cup chopped walnuts

Thaw frozen cranberries in refrigerator. Cream together butter and sugars. Beat in egg and vanilla. Sift together flour, baking soda and salt; stir into egg mixture. (Dough is very thick.) Fold in cranberries and walnuts. Spread carefully into pie shell. Bake at 350° for about 50 minutes or until pie tests done with a wooden pick. While pie bakes, blend topping ingredients until crumbly. Sprinkle topping over pie as soon as it's removed from oven; place an inverted bowl over pie and let steam 20 minutes. Serve warm or cooled. (You may omit topping and serve pie with whipped cream or ice cream, if desired.) **Yield:** 8 servings.

PUMPKIN CAKE ROLL
Sally Weaver, New Baden, Illinois

(PICTURED ON PAGE 70)

CAKE:
3 eggs
1 cup sugar
2/3 cup cooked pumpkin
1 teaspoon lemon juice
3/4 cup flour
1 teaspoon baking powder
2 teaspoons cinnamon
1 teaspoon ginger
1/2 teaspoon nutmeg
1/2 teaspoon salt
FILLING:
1 cup confectioners' sugar
2 packages (3 ounces *each*)
  cream cheese
4 tablespoons butter
1/2 teaspoon vanilla

To make cake, beat eggs in mixing bowl at high speed for 5 minutes; beat in sugar until blended. Stir in pumpkin and lemon juice. Combine flour, baking powder, spices and salt; fold into pumpkin mixture. Spread in greased and floured 15-in. x 10-in. x 1-in. jelly roll pan. Bake at 375° for 15 minutes. Remove cake from oven; turn out on clean linen towel liberally dusted with confectioners' sugar. Starting at narrow end, roll towel and cake together; cool. Make filling by combining ingredients and mixing until smooth. Unroll cooled cake; spread with filling to within 1 in. of edges. Roll back up; chill. Dust with additional confectioners' sugar before serving. **Yield:** 10-12 servings.

SOUTHERN PECAN
CHEESECAKE
Katherine Brown, Minot, North Dakota

(PICTURED ON PAGE 70)

CRUST:
1-1/2 cups quick oats
1/2 cup finely chopped pecans
1/2 cup brown sugar
1/3 cup melted butter
FILLING:
5 packages (8 ounces *each*)
  cream cheese, softened
1-2/3 cups light brown sugar
5 eggs
1 teaspoon vanilla
2 cups chopped pecans,
  divided

To make crust, place oats in food processor or blender; process to consistency of flour. Combine oats with remaining crust ingredients; press into bottom of 10-in. spring form pan. Chill. To make filling, beat cream cheese with mixer until fluffy; slowly add brown sugar and mix well. Add eggs, one at a time, mixing after each addition. Stir in vanilla and *half of nuts*. Mix and pour over crust. Bake at 350° for 1 hour; turn oven off but leave cake in oven for 30 minutes more. To reduce chance of cracks on top surface, run a knife around edge of cheesecake as soon as you remove it from the oven. Let cool to room temperature; chill 8 hours. Remove sides of pan. Press additional chopped pecans around sides and pipe top with whipped cream, if desired. **Yield:** 20-24 servings.

APPLE FRITTERS
Ruby Nelson, Mountain Home, Arkansas

(PICTURED ON PAGE 70)

1 beaten egg
1 cup milk
1 cup finely chopped *or* grated unpeeled cored apple
1/4 cup sugar
1/4 teaspoon salt
1 teaspoon grated orange peel
3 tablespoons orange juice
1/2 teaspoon vanilla
2 cups all-purpose flour
1 tablespoon baking powder
Vegetable oil for frying
Sifted confectioners' sugar

In mixing bowl, combine beaten egg, milk, chopped apple, sugar, salt, orange peel, juice and vanilla. Stir together flour and baking powder; fold into egg mixture, stirring just until all flour is moistened. Drop batter by rounded teaspoons into hot oil (350°). Fry until deep golden brown, about 3-4 minutes, turning once. Drain fritters thoroughly on paper towels. Roll in sugar or sift sugar over tops. **Yield:** About 40 fritters.

MEXICAN SANDWICHES
Dianne Mutcher, Brighton, Colorado

3 pounds ground beef
1 onion, chopped
1 package (10-12 ounces) longhorn cheese, grated
1 can (15 ounces) tomato sauce
1 can (4 ounces) chopped ripe olives
1 can (4 ounces) salsa
2 dozen hard rolls

Brown ground beef and onion together; drain. Add remaining ingredients except rolls. Pinch bread out of center of rolls; fill with the beef mixture. Wrap each roll in foil. Bake at 350° for 30 minutes. **Yield:** 2 dozen sandwiches.

MORE KITCHEN HINTS: To slice meat into thin strips for stroganoff or stir-fry, partially freeze meat first, to make cutting easier.

● Save the juices from your spiced fruits and other canned fruits—use them to pour over ham slices while baking.

● To freeze meatballs, place them on a cookie sheet until frozen. Place in a plastic bag and they'll stay separated so you can remove as many as you want at a time.

● Use greased muffin tins as holders when baking stuffed green peppers.

● Scissors are a great convenience for cutting celery and herbs—much better than using a knife.

● Don't use metal bowls for mixing salads—stick to wood, glass or china.

WESTERN MEAL IN ONE
Fern Wenger, Sabetha, Kansas

1 pound ground beef
1 tablespoon vegetable oil
1 clove garlic
1/2 cup chopped onion
1/2 cup chopped green pepper
1 teaspoon salt
1 teaspoon chili powder
1 can (16 ounces) red beans, *drained*
2-1/2 cups tomatoes with juice, chopped
3/4 cup uncooked rice
3/4 cup grated cheddar cheese
1/4 cup sliced black olives

Brown beef in vegetable oil with garlic. Add the onion and green pepper; cook until onion is transparent. Drain off fat. In a 2-qt. casserole, combine the meat mixture, salt, chili powder, beans, tomatoes and rice. Bake, covered, at 350° for 30 minutes. Uncover and sprinkle with cheese and olives; bake for 15 minutes more. **Yield:** 6-8 servings.

BARBECUED MUFFIN MEATBALLS
Janet Siciak, Bernardston, Massachusetts

SAUCE:
6 tablespoons brown sugar
1/2 cup catsup
1/4 teaspoon nutmeg
2 teaspoons dry mustard

MEATBALLS:
1 pound ground beef
1 pound ground pork
2 eggs
1-1/2 cups seasoned dry bread crumbs
1 teaspoon salt
1/2 teaspoon black pepper
2 tablespoons finely chopped onion

Combine sauce ingredients in a small bowl; set aside. Combine the meats, eggs, crumbs, salt, pepper, onion and *half* of sauce; mix gently until all ingredients are blended. Shape mixture into 12 balls and place in 3-in.-deep muffin pans. Make a small indentation in each ball and fill with remaining sauce. Bake at 400° for 30 minutes. **Yield:** 12 meatballs.

POLYNESIAN MEATBALLS
Marcia Baures, Waukesha, Wisconsin

MEATBALLS:
1-1/2 pounds ground chuck
2-1/2 ounces chopped water chestnuts
3/4 cup quick oatmeal
1/2 teaspoon garlic salt
1/2 teaspoon onion salt
1 egg, beaten
1/2 teaspoon soy sauce
1/2 cup milk

SAUCE:
1 cup brown sugar
1/2 cup beef bouillon
1/2 cup vinegar
2 tablespoons cornstarch
2 teaspoons soy sauce
1/2 cup pineapple juice
1 can (8-1/2 ounces) pineapple tidbits, *drained*
1/2 cup chopped green pepper

Combine meatball ingredients; shape into balls and brown in oil. Drain and set aside. Combine sauce ingredients *except* pineapple tidbits and green pepper; boil until thick. Stir in pineapple, green pepper and meatballs. Simmer for 30 minutes. **Yield:** 4 dozen meatballs.

CHILI RELLENO WONTON APPETIZERS
Susan Williams, Moapa, Nevada

2 pounds ground beef
2 onions, chopped
2 cups shredded
   cheddar cheese
1/2 teaspoon leaf oregano
1/2 teaspoon cumin
Dash garlic salt
1 can (4 ounces) chopped
   green chilies (add 1 more
   can for additional "zip"!)
1 package won ton wrappers

Brown and drain beef. Combine beef, onions, cheese, oregano, cumin, garlic salt and chilies. Place a spoonful of the meat mixture on each won ton wrapper and follow package directions for folding and sealing. Deep-fry 1-1/2 minutes or until golden; drain on paper towels. Serve warm. **Yield:** 6 dozen appetizers.

10-MINUTE MEAT LOAF
Carol Pilmer, Alliance, Ohio

1 pound ground beef
1 egg
1/2 cup bread crumbs
1/4 cup milk
2 tablespoons onion soup mix
2 tablespoons catsup
2 tablespoons soy sauce
1/2 cup shredded Swiss cheese

Combine all ingredients and shape into a round or oval loaf. Place in microwave-safe dish, cover with waxed paper and microwave on HIGH for 10 minutes, turning dish after 5 minutes of cooking. Drain and cover with foil. Let stand 10 minutes before slicing. **Yield:** 4-6 servings.

PIZZA CUPS
Kathy Lutz, Phillipsburg, Ohio

3/4 pound ground beef
1 can (6 ounces) tomato paste
1 tablespoon instant minced
   onion
1 teaspoon Italian seasoning
1/2 teaspoon salt
1 can (10 ounces) refrigerated
   biscuits
1/2 to 3/4 cup shredded
   mozzarella cheese

Brown and drain beef. Stir in tomato paste, onion and seasonings (mixture will be thick). Cook over low heat for 5 minutes, stirring frequently. Place biscuits in a greased muffin tin, pressing to cover bottom and sides. Spoon about 1/4 cup of meat mixture into biscuit-lined cups and sprinkle with cheese. Bake at 400° for 12 minutes or until golden brown. **Yield:** 12 pizza cups.

QUICK BAKED BEANS
Joey Mostowy, Bruin, Pennsylvania

3 to 4 strips bacon
1 clove garlic, minced
1 onion, chopped
1/2 green pepper, chopped
1/2 pound ground beef
Salt to taste
Black pepper to taste
1 can (1 pound) baked beans
2 hot dogs, sliced

Cook the bacon until crisp; set aside. Saute garlic, onion and green pepper in bacon drippings until golden. Add beef. Brown well; drain. Season with salt and pepper, if desired. Stir in beans and hot dogs; cover and simmer over low heat for 10 minutes. Crumble bacon over top and serve. **Yield:** 4-6 servings.

CHILI CON QUESO
Dixie Gaastra, Randolph, Wisconsin

1 pound ground beef
1/2 cup chopped green onion
3/4 cup chopped green pepper
1 can (8 ounces) tomato sauce
1 can (4 ounces) chopped
   green chilies
1 tablespoon Worcestershire
   sauce
1 package (1 pound)
   processed cheese spread,
   cubed
1 teaspoon ground red pepper
Paprika to taste
Unsalted corn chips

Brown beef and drain. In slow cooker, combine beef, onion, pepper, tomato sauce, chilies and Worcestershire sauce. Cover; cook on LOW for 2-3 hours. An hour before serving, add cheese, red pepper and paprika. Stir occasionally. **Quick stove-top method:** Brown beef and drain. Add remaining ingredients *except* corn chips. Simmer 1/2 hour, stirring occasionally. Serve with corn chips. **Yield:** 1-1/2 qts.

CHILI RELLENO BAKE
Jan Seibert, Albion, California

(PICTURED ON PAGE 72)

1/2 pound ground beef
1/2 pound chorizo or
   pork sausage
1 cup onion, chopped
2 cloves garlic, minced
   or pressed
2 cans (4 ounces *each*) whole
   green chilies, drained and
   seeded
2 cups shredded sharp
   cheddar cheese, *divided*
4 eggs
1/4 cup all-purpose flour,
   unsifted
1-1/2 cups milk
1/2 teaspoon salt
Tabasco sauce to taste

In a large skillet, crumble together the beef and chorizo or sausage. Cook over medium heat, stirring until meat is browned. Add onion and garlic; cook until onion is limp. Drain off fat. Line a 9-in. x 9-in. x 2-in. baking dish with half of the chilies; top with *1-1/2 cups* of the cheese. Add the meat mixture and top with remaining chilies; set aside. Beat together eggs and flour until smooth; add milk, salt, Tabasco. Blend well. Pour the egg mixture over casserole. Bake, uncovered, at 350° for about 40 minutes or until knife inserted off center comes out clean. Sprinkle remaining 1/2 cup cheese on top. Let stand 5 minutes before serving. **Yield:** 6 servings.

BARBECUED MEATBALLS
Connie Johnson, Friona, Texas

(PICTURED ON PAGE 72)

MEATBALLS:
3 pounds ground beef
1 can (12 ounces) evaporated
   milk
1 cup oatmeal
1 cup cracker crumbs
2 eggs
1/2 cup chopped onion
1/2 teaspoon garlic powder
2 teaspoons salt
1/2 teaspoon pepper
2 teaspoons chili powder
SAUCE:
2 cups catsup
1 cup brown sugar
1/2 teaspoon liquid smoke or
   to taste
1/2 teaspoon garlic powder
1/4 cup chopped onion

To make meatballs, combine all ingredients (mixture will be soft) and shape into walnut-size balls. Place meatballs in a single layer on wax paper-lined cookie sheets; freeze until solid. Store frozen meatballs in freezer bags until ready to cook. To make sauce, combine all ingredients and stir until sugar is dissolved. Place frozen meatballs in a 13-in. x 9-in. x 2-in. baking pan; pour on the sauce. Bake at 350° for 1 hour. **Yield:** 80 meatballs.

BLACK BEAN CHILI SALAD
Carmen Gratton, New Smyrna Beach, Florida

(PICTURED ON PAGE 72)

✓ This tasty dish uses less sugar, salt and fat. Recipe includes *Diabetic Exchanges*.

- 1 package (12 ounces) black beans
- 2 cups chopped onion, *divided*
- 12 cloves chopped garlic, *divided*
- 2 cans (20 ounces *each*) whole tomatoes, chopped, undrained
- 1 pound ground beef
- 1 green pepper, chopped
- 1 teaspoon salt
- 1 teaspoon black pepper
- 2 tablespoons chili powder
- 1-1/2 tablespoons ground cumin
- 1/8 teaspoon crushed red pepper

ACCOMPANIMENTS:
Tortilla chips
- 1 cup grated cheddar cheese
- 1 cup thinly sliced lettuce
- 1 mashed avocado
- 1/2 cup sour cream

In large cast-iron pot, cover the black beans with water and bring to a boil. Turn off heat; let the beans soak for at least 4 hours. Turn on heat; add 1-1/2 cups onions and 8 cloves garlic; simmer until beans are tender. Drain liquid from beans. (Beans can be cooked in advance and frozen until needed.) Add tomatoes to beans and cook on low heat. Meanwhile, brown ground beef in skillet with remaining onion, green pepper, 4 cloves garlic, salt, pepper, chili powder, cumin and red pepper. Drain off fat and add meat mixture to beans and tomatoes. Heat through. Serve on individual plates garnished with accompaniments, as desired. **Diabetic Exchanges:** One serving equals 3 protein, 2 bread, 2 vegetable, 2 fat; also 394 calories, 550 mg sodium, 73 mg cholesterol, 41 gm carbohydrate, 28 gm protein, 18 gm fat. **Yield:** 8 servings.

SHANGHAI NOODLES WITH SPICY BEEF SAUCE
Ena Quiggle, Goodhue, Minnesota

(PICTURED ON PAGE 72)

- 3 tablespoons vegetable *or* peanut oil
- 2 teaspoons minced garlic
- 1-1/2 teaspoons minced fresh gingerroot
- 1/4 teaspoon crushed red pepper *or* to taste
- 1-1/2 cups chopped onion
- 1 pound ground beef
- 1/2 cup chicken broth, *divided*
- 1/3 cup hoisin* sauce
- 1/4 cup soy sauce
- 1/4 cup dry sherry *or* beef broth
- 2 tablespoons cornstarch
- 16 ounces vermicelli noodles, cooked and drained
- 2 tablespoons toasted sesame oil
- 1/2 cup diagonally sliced green onions

Heat wok or large skillet until hot; add the oil, garlic, gingerroot and pepper flakes. Saute about 5 seconds. Add onion; stir-fry until onion is transparent. Crumble in ground beef; stir-fry until the meat is light brown. In a small bowl, combine *1/4 cup* chicken broth, hoisin sauce, soy sauce and sherry/broth. Stir into meat mixture. Cover, reduce heat and simmer 10 minutes, stirring once or twice. Meanwhile, dissolve cornstarch in remaining chicken broth. Slowly stir into meat mixture; cook and stir until the sauce is thick. In separate bowl, combine the hot vermicelli and sesame oil. Pour sauce over top; toss gently to combine. Serve topped with the green onions. *Hoisin sauce can be found in the Oriental section of most supermarkets. **Yield:** 4-6 servings.

BEEF CASSEROLE ITALIANO
Susan Longyear, Washington, Virginia

(PICTURED ON PAGE 73)

- 1 pound ground beef
- 1/4 cup chopped yellow onion
- 2 cans (8 ounces *each*) tomato sauce
- 1 teaspoon parsley flakes
- 1/2 teaspoon leaf oregano
- 1 teaspoon leaf basil
- 1/2 teaspoon salt, *divided*
- 1/4 teaspoon pepper

- 2 packages (10 ounces each) frozen chopped spinach, *thawed and drained well*
- 2 cups ricotta cheese
- 1 package (8 ounces) mozzarella cheese slices

Brown ground beef and onion; drain off fat. Stir in the tomato sauce, parsley, oregano, basil, *1/4 teaspoon* salt and pepper. Simmer, uncovered, for 10 minutes, stirring occasionally. Meanwhile, combine spinach, ricotta cheese and remaining 1/4 teaspoon salt. Spoon spinach mixture around edges of 13-in. x 9-in. x 2-in. baking dish; pour beef mixture into center. Cut each mozzarella slice into three strips and arrange in a lattice pattern over meat. Bake at 375° for 20 minutes. **Yield:** 8 servings.

SUNDAY SUPPER SOUP
Margaret Gage, Roseboom, New York

(PICTURED ON PAGE 73)

MEATBALLS:
- 1-1/2 pounds ground beef
- 1 egg, slightly beaten
- 3 tablespoons water
- 1/2 cup dry bread crumbs
- 1/4 teaspoon salt
- 1 tablespoon chopped parsley
- 2 tablespoons butter

SOUP:
- 2 cups water
- 1 can (10-1/2 ounces) condensed beef broth, *undiluted*
- 1 can (1 pound, 12 ounces) tomatoes, *undrained, chopped*
- 1 envelope (1-3/8 ounces) dry onion soup mix
- 1 cup sliced carrots
- 1/4 cup chopped celery tops
- 1/4 cup chopped parsley
- 1/4 teaspoon black pepper
- 1/4 teaspoon dried oregano leaves
- 1/4 teaspoon dried basil leaves
- 1 bay leaf

To make the meatballs, combine beef, egg, water, bread crumbs, salt and parsley. Mix lightly; shape into 24 balls. In 5-qt. Dutch oven, melt butter and brown meatballs, a single layer at a time, on all sides. Drain off fat; remove meatballs and set aside. To make soup, combine ingredients in same Dutch oven. Bring to boiling. Reduce heat; cover and simmer for 20 minutes. Add meatballs; simmer 20 minutes longer. **Yield:** 6-8 servings, about 2 qts.

TACO TARTLETS
LaVonne Hartel, Williston, North Dakota

(PICTURED ON PAGE 73)

MEAT SHELLS:
- 1 pound ground beef
- 2 tablespoons taco seasoning mix
- 2 tablespoons ice water

FILLING:
- 1 cup dairy sour cream
- 2 tablespoons red taco sauce
- 2 ounces chopped ripe olives
- 1 cup coarsely crushed tortilla chips, *divided*
- 1/2 cup shredded cheddar cheese

To make meat shells, combine ingredients; mix well. Press meat mixture into bottom and sides of tiny tart pans and set aside. Combine sour cream, taco sauce, olives and *3/4 cup* tortilla chips. Spoon filling into each shell, mounding slightly. Combine remaining chips and cheese; sprinkle over each tartlet. Bake at 375° for 10 minutes. Garnish with taco sauce. **Yield:** 32 tartlets.

TAMALE PIE
Naomi Giddis, Grawn, Michigan

(PICTURED ON PAGE 73)

 This tasty dish uses less sugar, salt and fat. Recipe includes *Diabetic Exchanges.*

FILLING:
- 1 pound ground beef
- 1 cup chopped onion
- 1 green pepper, chopped
- 1 can (15 ounces) tomato sauce
- 1 can (28 ounces) tomatoes, cut up
- 1 can (17 ounces) whole kernel corn, drained
- 1/2 cup sliced pitted ripe olives
- 1 clove garlic, minced
- 1 tablespoon sugar
- 1/2 teaspoon salt
- 2 teaspoons chili powder
- Dash black pepper
- 1 cup grated cheddar cheese

CRUST:
- 3/4 cup yellow cornmeal
- 1/2 teaspoon salt
- 2 cups cold water
- 1/2 teaspoon chili powder
- 1 tablespoon butter

To make filling, brown ground beef, onions and green pepper; drain. Add the remaining ingredients except for cheese. Bring to boil; simmer, uncovered, for 20 minutes or until thickened. Add the cheese; stir until melted. Set aside. To make crust, combine cornmeal, salt, water and chili powder in saucepan. Cook on medium-high, stirring constantly, until thick. Add butter; mix well. Spread half of crust mixture over bottom of a 12-in. x 8-in. x 2-in. baking dish. (Note: Recipe is pictured in 9-in. square dish.) Add filling; spoon on the remaining crust. Bake at 375° for 45 minutes. Top with 1/2 cup of grated cheese, if desired. **Diabetic Exchanges:** One serving equals 2 protein, 2 bread, 1 vegetable, 2 fat; also, 379 calories, 1,255 mg sodium, 93 mg cholesterol, 32 gm carbohydrate, 25 gm protein, 18 gm fat. **Yield:** 6 servings.

CRESCENT CHEESEBURGER PIE
Elinore Dumont, Drumheller, Alberta

(PICTURED ON PAGE 74)

- 1 pound ground beef
- 1/2 cup chopped onion
- 1 can (8 ounces) tomato sauce
- 1 can (4 ounces) chopped mushrooms, drained
- 1/4 cup chopped parsley
- 1/4 teaspoon salt
- 1/4 teaspoon dried oregano, crushed
- 1/8 teaspoon pepper
- 2 packages (8 rolls *each*) refrigerated crescent rolls
- 3 eggs
- 6 slices (6 ounces) American cheese
- 1 tablespoon water

Brown the ground beef and onion until onion is transparent; drain off fat. Stir in tomato sauce, mushrooms, parsley, salt, oregano and pepper; set aside. Unroll 1 package of rolls and separate dough into triangles. In lightly greased 9-in. pie plate, arrange triangles with pointed ends to the center and press edges together to form a pie shell. Separate eggs; beat together whites from 3 eggs plus yolks from *2* eggs. Pour *half* of beaten egg mixture over pie shell. Spoon meat mixture into shell; arrange cheese slices on top. Spread with remaining beaten egg. Mix reserved egg yolk with water and set aside. Unroll second package of rolls; place four sections of dough together to form a 12-in. x 6-in. rectangle. Press edges and perforations together; roll dough into a 12-in. square. Brush edges of bottom crust with egg yolk/water mixture; place dough on top of filling. Trim; seal and flute edges. Cut slits in top crust. Brush top with the remaining egg yolk/water mixture. Loosely cover edge with foil strip to prevent over-browning. Bake at 350° for 20 minutes; cover center of pie loosely with foil and bake 20 minutes longer. Let stand 10 minutes before serving. **Yield:** 6 servings.

MEXICAN LASAGNA
Jeanne Bennett, Minden, Louisiana

(PICTURED ON PAGE 74)

- 1-1/2 pounds ground beef
- 1-1/2 teaspoons ground cumin
- 1 tablespoon chili powder
- 1/4 teaspoon garlic powder
- 1/4 teaspoon red pepper
- 1 teaspoon salt *or* to taste
- 1 teaspoon black pepper *or* to taste
- 1 can (16 ounces) tomatoes, chopped
- 10 to 12 corn tortillas
- 2 cups small curd cottage cheese, *drained*
- 1 cup grated Monterey Jack cheese with peppers
- 1 egg
- 1/2 cup grated cheddar cheese
- 2 cups shredded lettuce
- 1/2 cup chopped tomatoes
- 3 green onions, chopped
- 1/4 cup sliced black olives

Brown ground beef; drain thoroughly. Add cumin, chili powder, garlic powder, red pepper, salt, black pepper and tomatoes; heat through. Cover bottom and sides of a 13-in. x 9-in. x 2-in. baking dish with tortillas. Pour beef mixture over tortillas; place a layer of tortillas over meat mixture and set aside. Combine cottage cheese, Monterey Jack cheese and egg; pour over tortillas. Bake at 350° for 30 minutes. Remove from oven; sprinkle rows of cheddar cheese, lettuce, tomatoes, green onions and olives diagonally across center of casserole. **Yield:** 6-8 servings.

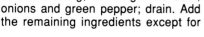

KOREAN BEEF PATTIES

Marsha Ransom, South Haven, Michigan

(PICTURED ON PAGE 74)

1 pound ground beef
4 tablespoons soy sauce
2 tablespoons sugar
1 tablespoon toasted sesame seeds, crushed
1 tablespoon toasted sesame oil
2-1/2 tablespoons chopped green onion
1 tablespoon garlic, minced
Black pepper to taste

Combine all ingredients. Form into four balls and flatten into patties. Broil, grill or pan-fry until done. **Yield:** 4 servings.

ITALIAN VEGETABLE SOUP

Bonnie Vawter, Alton, Missouri

(PICTURED ON PAGE 74)

 This tasty dish uses less sugar, salt and fat. Recipe includes *Diabetic Exchanges*.

1 pound ground beef
1 cup diced onion
1 cup sliced celery
1 cup sliced carrots
2 cloves garlic, *minced*
1 can (16 ounces) tomatoes
1 can (15 ounces) tomato sauce
1 can (15 ounces) red kidney beans, *undrained*
2 cups water
5 teaspoons beef bouillon granules
1 tablespoon dried parsley flakes
1 teaspoon salt
1/2 teaspoon oregano
1/2 teaspoon sweet basil
1/4 teaspoon black pepper
2 cups shredded cabbage
1 cup frozen *or* fresh green beans, cut in 1-inch pieces, *optional*
1/2 cup small elbow macaroni
Parmesan cheese

Brown beef in large heavy kettle; drain. Add all the ingredients *except* cabbage, green beans and macaroni. Bring to boil. Lower heat; cover and simmer 20 minutes. Add cabbage, green beans and macaroni; bring to boil and simmer until vegetables are tender. If you prefer a thinner soup, add additional water or broth. Sprinkle with the Parmesan cheese before serving. **Diabetic Exchanges:**

One serving equals 1 protein, 1 bread; also 152 calories, 776 mg sodium, 34 mg cholesterol, 17 gm carbohydrate, 12 gm protein, 4 gm fat. **Yield:** 12 servings.

SALMON/CUCUMBER APPETIZER

Kay Schumacker, Batesville, Indiana

2 packages (3 ounces *each*) cream cheese
1/2 teaspoon salt
1/2 teaspoon dill weed
2 medium cucumbers, cut into 1/8-inch slices
1 can (16 ounces) red salmon, *drained, deboned*
Pimiento

Combine cream cheese, salt and dill weed; mix until blended. Using a pastry bag with large star tip, pipe a star of cream cheese mixture onto each cucumber slice. Top each star with a small piece of salmon; garnish with a tiny piece of pimiento. Cover with plastic wrap; store in the refrigerator until ready to serve. **Yield:** About 2 dozen appetizers.

CRAB DELIGHTS

Marie Schomas, Homewood, Illinois

9 slices white bread
1 can (7-1/2 ounces) crab meat, *flaked*
1 small onion, grated
1 cup grated cheddar cheese
1 cup mayonnaise
1 teaspoon curry powder
1/2 teaspoon salt

Remove crusts from bread; cut each slice into 4 squares, strips or triangles. Mix remaining ingredients; spread on bread. Place on cookie sheet; broil till golden and bubbly. **Yield:** 36 appetizers.

MEAT & CHEESE COCKTAIL ROUNDS

Lisa Seaba, Muscatine, Iowa

1 pound *lean* ground beef
1 pound Italian sausage
1 pound processed American cheese, *cubed*
Garlic powder to taste
1 package party rye bread
Leaf oregano, *crumbled*

Brown meats together in large skillet; drain off fat. Add cheese and garlic powder; simmer until cheese melts, stirring to blend. Spread meat/cheese mixture on rye bread rounds, using 1 teaspoon for each slice. Sprinkle with oregano. Bake at 375° for 15 minutes and serve hot. (You can also cool and freeze flat on cookie sheets until firm; transfer to heavy plastic freezer bags. To reheat, microwave on 70% power for 1 minute.) **Yield:** 68 appetizers.

ROASTED QUAIL WITH WHITE WINE SAUCE

Jordan Hollow Farm Inn
Stanley, Virginia

1 package (6 oz.) Uncle Ben's Long Grain and Wild Rice
1 apple, peeled, cored and cubed
3 small carrots, cubed
12 quail (2 per person)
3 tablespoons soy sauce
1 teaspoon garlic powder
1 teaspoon dried tarragon
1/8 teaspoon finely ground rosemary
1 cup flour
1/4 cup grated Parmesan cheese
1/4 cup peanut oil
SAUCE:
1/4 cup white wine (Chablis or other dry or semidry)
1 teaspoon chicken stock base
1/8 teaspoon white pepper
2 cups heavy cream

Preheat oven to 400°. Add apple and carrot cubes to rice and cook according to package directions. Season quail inside and out with soy sauce and half the garlic powder, tarragon and rosemary. Stuff each bird with the rice mixture, reserving the remaining rice.

Mix flour, Parmesan cheese and remaining herbs and roll each quail lightly in the mixture. Saute in peanut oil until lightly browned. Place in preheated oven and roast for 8 to 15 minutes, until juice runs clear when breast is pierced. Arrange remaining rice on platter, place quail on top, and keep warm.

Pour off all but two tablespoons of oil from the saute pan. Add wine, stirring to loosen pan drippings. Add chicken base, white pepper and cream; simmer until thickened. Pour over quail, garnish with two tablespoons fresh chopped parsley or other herbs. **Yield:** 6 servings.

COUNTRY INNS

Chalet de France

Star Route, Box 20-A, Kneeland, California 95549

Phone: 1-707/443-6512 or 707/444-3144

Directions: From Eureka, California, the Chalet de France is a 22-mile (45-minute) scenic drive. The Vieryas provide a detailed map if requested in advance. Airport pick-up can be arranged for an additional charge.

Innkeepers: Liliane and Doug Vierya

Schedule: Open year-round. (If you're snowed-in while there, the additional stay is free!)

Accommodations and Rates: Two rooms with shared bath, American plan, $180-$195 per couple per day includes all meals, beverages and activities. Bed and breakfast, $97 per couple with full gourmet breakfast. Payable in full at time of reservation; no credit cards. No smoking, children or pets. Wheelchair access: possible.

Only the view and hospitality beat the food at the Chalet de France, where lunchtime on the deck finds guests relishing chicken salad, croissants, sliced tomatoes, hard-boiled eggs and upside-down caramel custard.

The evening meal could begin with savory appetizers such as smoked salmon mousse, chicken liver pate, stuffed mushrooms, mushroom brie and sausage-filled puff pastry tarts...followed by cream of leek soup, rack of lamb, potatoes roasted in garlic and zucchini/tomato/onion casserole. Desserts can be as simple as pecan tassies or as elaborate as Lili's homemade cheesecake, decorated with white-chocolate dipped strawberries and green chocolate leaves.

Here is a sampling of the elegant, delicious food served at the Chalet de France:

CHICKEN LIVER PATE

1/4 cup butter
1/2 pound chicken livers, halved, membrane removed
3 oz. chopped fresh mushrooms (about 7 whole)
2 tablespoons chopped green onions or shallots
1 tablespoon chopped parsley
1/4 teaspoon crushed thyme
Dash salt
1 tablespoon brandy
1/4 cup Madeira wine
1/2 cup butter, cut in pieces
1/2 can chopped black olives (4-1/4-oz. can)

Melt 1/4 cup butter in frying pan over medium heat. Add next six ingredients and cook, stirring until livers are brown on all sides and well done. Warm brandy, pour over liver and ignite, shaking pan until flame dies. Add wine, simmer briefly. Put liver mixture in blender and puree with 1/2 cup butter. (Add a few pieces at a time. If the mixture seems too dry, add more wine.) Blend until smooth; remove from blender. Fold in the drained olives; pour into one large or several individual terrines. Chill until firm, several hours or overnight. Serve with crusty French bread or crackers. This pate keeps 2-3 days if refrigerated and covered. **Yield:** 2 cups.

TEATIME TASSIES

PASTRY:
1 3-ounce package of cream cheese (room temperature)
1/2 cup butter (room temperature)
1 cup flour
FILLING:
2 eggs
1-1/2 cups brown sugar
2 tablespoons soft butter
2 teaspoons vanilla extract
1-1/4 cups coarsely chopped pecans
24 pecan halves

Blend cream cheese with butter, stir in flour. Chill for about 1 hour. Shape dough in 24 1-inch balls and line mini muffin cups on bottom and side. Use more dough if you use small tart shells. To make the filling, combine eggs, sugar, butter and vanilla and beat until smooth. A dash of salt may be added. Divide the chopped pecans among the cups, add egg mixture and place half a pecan on top of each cup. Bake at 325°

for about 25 minutes or until filling is set. Cool and remove from pan carefully. As a variation, you may add 2 ounces of melted semi-sweet chocolate to the filling. **Yield:** 24 pastries.

SMOKED SALMON MOUSSE

1 tablespoon finely chopped shallots or green onions
2 tablespoons unsalted butter
2-3 ounces smoked salmon, boned and flaked
1/4 cup cream cheese
1/4 cup sour cream
1/4 cup unsalted butter, softened
2 tablespoons lemon juice
1 tablespoon vodka, optional
1/4 cup whipping cream, whipped

Saute shallots in 2 tablespoons butter until golden; add salmon, stir and remove from heat. Place mixture in blender; add cream cheese, sour cream and softened butter; blend well. Add lemon juice and vodka; blend until smooth. Remove mixture to a bowl and fold in whipped cream. Refrigerate several hours or up to 2 days. Serve chilled, but not too cold, on crackers or warm French bread. **Yield:** 2-1/2 cups.

STUFFED MUSHROOMS

24 large mushrooms (1-1/2 to 2 inches)—2 packages (8 ounces)
3 to 4 small green onions
2 sprigs of parsley
4 to 6 tablespoons butter
4 to 6 tablespoons sherry
2 to 3 ounces cream cheese, room temperature

Wash and dry the mushrooms and remove stems. Chop stems, onions and parsley. Saute in 2-3 tablespoons of the butter until light brown; add 3 tablespoons of the sherry. Continue cooking until most of the liquid has evaporated. Remove from heat and add to cream cheese. Mix well; set aside. Lightly saute mushroom caps in remaining 2-3 tablespoons butter; add 2 tablespoons of sherry. *Do not overcook.* Remove mushrooms from pan. When cool enough to handle, fill with a generous amount of the cheese filling and place in baking dish. When ready to serve, heat in a 325° oven for 10 to 15 minutes. Sprinkle with paprika and chopped fresh parsley; serve while hot. **Yield:** 8 appetizer servings.

BEST COOK

Variety is the spice of life, and Helen Kubisiak enjoys spicing up her family's meals with menus that range from down-home country dishes to German/Russian regional fare to Oriental experiments!

"Mom grew up during the Depression, when food was scarce," wrote her daughter, Karen. "Her own mother managed to come up with inexpensive but great-tasting meals. Mom watched closely and remembered how to prepare many different types of foods."

Ethnic specialties remembered from childhood are an important part of Helen's cooking, according to Karen. "Mom comes from a German/Russian background and Dad's Polish/German. So dough dishes like cheese buttons and fleishkeuchle are part of our family tradition.

"And at Christmas, Mom serves smoked turkey, German and American potato salad, dinner rolls and her traditional pfefferneuse cookies and 7-layer Icelandic cake. Oh, what a treat!

"But Mom likes to experiment. She creates any American dish we might be craving...also Mexican specialties like tacos and enchiladas...and even Oriental favorites such as pork chow mein and sukiyaki—all without using a cookbook!"

"I enjoy cooking for my family, as well as preparing large feasts for our friends," Helen told us. "And I especially like the challenge of making ethnic dishes.

"Anyone can be a good cook if they watch other cooks, read cookbooks thoroughly...and have fun experimenting!"

HELEN'S TOFFEE SQUARES

1 cup butter, softened to room temperature
1 cup brown sugar
1 egg yolk
2 teaspoons vanilla
1-7/8 cups all-purpose flour
6 milk chocolate bars (1.65 ounces each)
1 cup chopped toasted almonds or pecans

In mixing bowl, cream together butter and brown sugar until light-colored and fluffy. Add egg yolk and vanilla; gradually beat in flour until smooth and blended. (Dough will be thick.) Spread evenly on ungreased 16-in. x 14-in. x 1-in. baking pan. Bake at 350° for 15 minutes or until crust is golden brown and puffy. Remove from oven. Arrange unwrapped chocolate bars evenly over surface of crust; let stand for 5 minutes to soften. Spread chocolate evenly over crust; sprinkle with chopped nuts. Cool; cut into squares. **Yield:** 40 squares.

TWENTY-FOUR-HOUR COLESLAW SALAD

1 medium head cabbage, shredded
1 small onion, finely chopped
1 green pepper, finely chopped
6 stuffed olives, chopped
1/2 cup granulated sugar
DRESSING:
1/2 cup white vinegar
1/2 teaspoon salt
1 teaspoon celery seed or caraway seed
1/8 teaspoon black pepper
1/2 cup vegetable oil

Prepare vegetables; place in large bowl. Sprinkle with sugar; *do not mix.* Combine dressing ingredients in saucepan; boil for 2 minutes. Add dressing to cabbage. Refrigerate, covered, overnight. Stir well before serving. **Yield:** 8-10 servings.

PINEAPPLE CHEESE MOLD

1 envelope unflavored gelatin
3/4 cup sugar
3/4 cup pineapple juice
1 can (9 ounces) crushed pineapple
1 cup shredded American cheese
1 cup heavy whipping cream, *whipped*

Dissolve gelatin and sugar in pineapple juice in small saucepan. Bring to a boil. Remove from heat; chill until partially set. Add crushed pineapple, shredded cheese and whipped cream to gelatin base, mixing thoroughly but gently. Pour into oiled 3-1/2 cup mold. Refrigerate until firm. Unmold on bed of greens. **Yield:** 6-8 servings.

CHILI CON QUESO DIP

1/2 cup chopped onion
1 tablespoon butter or margarine
1 tablespoon flour
1 can (10 ounces) tomatoes and green chili peppers, (I use El Paso or Ashley's)
1/2 pound diced processed cheese spread
1 tablespoon salsa ranchera or 3 to 4 drops Tabasco sauce
Tortilla chips

In large skillet, saute onions in butter/margarine. Add flour; mix well. Add tomatoes and green chili peppers. Cook mixture. When sauce begins to thicken, add diced cheese. Cook over low heat, mixing well, until cheese is melted. Stir in salsa or Tabasco sauce. Serve hot in chafing dish with chips. **Yield:** About 2 cups.

THOUSAND ISLAND DRESSING

2 cups mayonnaise
1/2 cup catsup
1 small onion, minced
1 medium green pepper, diced
4 hard cooked eggs, diced
Few drops Tabasco sauce or to taste

Mix all ingredients together; chill. Serve over lettuce. **Yield:** About 1 quart.

Light the candles, turn up the carols and put the finishing touches on your Christmas Eve buffet. After weeks of anticipation and hours of preparation, it's finally time to enjoy the warmth and love of a family Christmas.

Gather family and friends around a sparkling table filled with holiday favorites. Sample such distinctive ethnic dishes as cheese- or potato-stuffed Pierogi, tomato- and cheese-drenched Mostaccioli and spiced and sauced Swedish Meatballs...filled with the traditional flavors that link generations.

Expand your holiday horizons with regional favorites such as Crab Pie, Oyster Cheese Appetizer Log, Christmas Vegetable Salad and Fresh Cranberry Punch.

CANDLELIGHT FEAST: Clockwise on table from lower left—**Oyster Cheese Appetizer Log,** Mrs. William Tracy, Jerseyville, Illinois (Pg. 91); **Christmas Vegetable Salad,** Mary Dean, Eau Claire, Wisconsin (Pg. 91); **Celery En Casserole,** Mary Lou Sipherd, Bishop, California (Pg. 91); **Fresh Cranberry Punch,** Deanna House, Portage, Michigan (Pg. 91); **Swedish Meatballs,** Emily Gould, Hawarden, Iowa (Pg. 92); **Mostaccioli,** Nancy Mundhenke, Kinsley, Kansas (Pg. 91); **Polish Pierogi,** Adeline Piscitelli, Sayreville, New Jersey (Pg. 91); **Swiss 'n' Crab Supper Pie,** Kathy Crow, Cordova, Alaska (Pg. 92).

Yuletide Bone China courtesy of Pfaltzgraff.

Help yourself to desserts rich with nostalgic tastes of Christmases past. Try lacy Scandinavian Krumkake that crumbles delightfully on the tongue or delicate Shortbread cookies with a crisp, buttery bite. These old country favorites are treasured holiday traditions.

For a sweet treat, there's a Christmas citrus compote appropriately named Orange Appeal, and White Christmas Candy with red and green peppermint crunch that looks and tastes like Christmas!

Enjoy...and happy holidays!

SUGARPLUMS: Clockwise from lower left—**Orange Appeal,** Billie Moss, El Sobrante, California; **Shortbread,** Mrs. Allen Swenson, Camdenton, Missouri; **Whipped Cream Krumkake,** Imelda Nesteby, Decorah, Iowa; **White Christmas Candy,** Carol Hammond, Helena, Alabama. (All recipes can be found on page 92.)

Recipes from Linnea Rein, Topeka, Kansas

MEALS IN MINUTES

WHEN LEFTOVERS from holiday feasts seem overwhelming, here's a way to turn today's turkey into tomorrow's speedy meal!

These hot and hearty turkey burritos are a tasty way to use up that cooked turkey. And the side dish offers a quick-cooking complement to the burritos. This take-off on Spanish rice uses tomato juice instead of water or broth for cooking the instant rice. If you like a snappier taste, just stir some picante sauce into the cooked rice.

Stirring up some other leftovers—cranberry sauce and yogurt—results in a fast dessert that's sure to be a family favorite. Layer the sauce and yogurt together in clear glass dishes for a pretty look, and top it with granola for crunch. (This combination also makes a quick, nutritious, on-the-go breakfast!)

When your kitchen fare has to be fast, turn that turkey into a time-saver!

TURKEY SALAD BURRITOS

        2 cups chopped cooked turkey
    3/4 cup finely chopped celery
    1/2 cup finely chopped onion
    1/4 to 1/2 cup sliced black olives
        1 cup shredded cheddar
            cheese
    1/2 cup salad dressing
            or mayonnaise
    1/2 cup picante sauce
    1/2 teaspoon salt
        6 soft 7-8-in. flour tortillas
Picante sauce
Black olives for garnish

In medium mixing bowl, combine turkey, celery, onion, black olives and cheese. In another bowl, whisk together salad dressing, picante sauce and salt. Pour sauce over turkey mixture; blend well. Spoon filling onto tortillas; wrap burrito-

style as pictured. Heat in 13-in. x 9-in. x 3-in. baking pan at 350° for 20 minutes or until thoroughly warmed or microwave each burrito 2 to 2-1/2 min-

utes on HIGH. Serve with additional picante sauce; garnish with black olives. **Yield:** 4 servings.

CONFETTI RICE

        2 cups tomato juice
        1 cup frozen mixed vegetables,
            broken apart
    1-1/2 cups instant rice
    1/8 teaspoon pepper

Combine tomato juice and mixed vegetables in medium saucepan; bring to a boil. Stir in rice and pepper. Cover, turn off heat and allow to stand 6 minutes. Fluff with fork. **Yield:** 4 servings.

CRANBERRY/YOGURT PARFAITS

    3/4 cup whole berry cranberry
            sauce
        2 cups plain yogurt
    1/2 cup granola, homemade
            or purchased

Place about 2 tablespoons cranberry sauce in bottom of 4 parfait glasses. Layer yogurt, remaining cranberry sauce and granola on top. **Yield:** 4 servings.

Have this dressing on hand when you'd like a tossed salad to accompany your burritos.

FRESH BASIL AND GARLIC DRESSING

Glacier Bay Country Inn
Gustavus, Alaska

        1 ripe, medium-sized tomato,
            cut in wedges
    1/2 cup olive oil
    1/3 cup red wine vinegar
    1/4 cup crushed basil
    1/4 cup chopped chives
        2 cloves fresh garlic
    1/2 teaspoon salt
    1/2 teaspoon white pepper

Combine all ingredients in blender; process until smooth. Refrigerate for several hours to blend flavors before serving. **Yield:** 1-1/4 cups.

Christmas means many things in country kitchens—foremost among them is festive candy!

As a taste-topping treat for family and friends or gaily wrapped for gift giving, holiday sweets take the form of easy microwave candies... flavorful fruit...elegant hand-dipped chocolates...plus everything in between.

Here's a selection that's sure to satisfy a sweet tooth. It's the best of the season...to all of you!

SWEETS FOR THE SEASON. Clockwise from lower left: **Orange Sugared Pecans,** Murri Mills, Brady, Texas (Pg. 93); **Stuffed Dates,** Dorothy Pepper, Thermal, California (Pg. 93); **Chocolate Almond Truffles,** Arla Railsback, New Richmond, Wisconsin (Pg. 93); **Two-Tone Fudge,** Lavonne Sullivan, Topeka, Kansas (Pg. 93); **Microwave Leche Quemada,** Mildred Kneupper, New Braunfels, Texas (Pg. 94); **Spiced Mixed Nuts,** Joanne Warner, Baldwin, Wisconsin (Pg. 93); **Orange/Chocolate Sugarplums,** Evelyn Skaggs, Nixa, Missouri (Pg. 93); **Candied Citrus Peels,** Mary Malinowski, Lee Center, New York (Pg. 94).

Sweet surprises mean so much when they're handmade in your own country kitchen. Whether you are concocting candies to give as gifts or for treating guests, these four are sure to be festive favorites.

The name says it all for Aunt Rose's Fantastic Butter Toffee. And the nuts in rich Macadamia Nut Fudge make an exotic change-of-taste.

Mounds Balls are a familiar combination of coconut and dark chocolate. And until you make Easy Microwave Caramels yourself, you won't believe it can be this simple to make mouth-watering caramels.

Mmmm...homemade candy—how sweet it is!

COUNTRY CONFECTIONS: Clockwise from top jar—**Aunt Rose's Fantastic Butter Toffee,** Rosie Kimberlin, Los Angeles, California (Pg. 94); **Macadamia Nut Fudge,** Vicki Fioranelli, Cleveland, Mississippi (Pg. 95); **Mounds Balls,** Kathy Dorman, Snover, Michigan (Pg. 94) **Easy Microwave Caramels,** Darleen Worm, Fond Du Lac, Wisconsin, (Pg. 94).

CELERY EN CASSEROLE
Mary Lou Sipherd, Bishop, California

(PICTURED ON PAGE 84)

4-1/2 cups diagonally sliced celery
1 can (5 ounces) drained water
    chestnuts, sliced
1/4 cup diced pimiento
1/4 cup slivered almonds
1 can (10-1/2 ounces) cream of
    chicken soup
TOPPING:
1/2 cup dry bread crumbs
4 teaspoons melted butter
2 tablespoons sesame seed
2 tablespoons Parmesan cheese

Cook celery in water for 5 minutes or until tender/crisp. Drain; add water chestnuts, pimiento, almonds and soup. Pour into 1-1/2-qt. buttered baking dish. Combine topping ingredients; sprinkle over top of casserole. Bake at 350° for 25 minutes or until crumbs are golden brown. **Yield:** 8 servings.

FRESH CRANBERRY PUNCH
Deanna House, Portage, Michigan

(PICTURED ON PAGE 85)

4 cups fresh or frozen
    cranberries
3-1/2 quarts water
12 whole cloves
4 sticks cinnamon (3 in. each)
3/4 cup orange juice
2/3 cup fresh lemon juice
2 cups sugar

In Dutch oven or large kettle, combine cranberries, water, cloves and cinnamon. Bring to boil; cover, reduce heat and simmer 12-15 minutes. Strain cooked juice through fine sieve or cheese cloth, squeezing gently. To strained juice, add orange juice, lemon juice and sugar; stir until sugar dissolves. Serve piping hot. **Yield:** 25 1/2-cup servings.

OYSTER CHEESE APPETIZER LOG
Mrs. William Tracy, Jerseyville, Illinois

(PICTURED ON PAGE 84)

3 packages (8 ounces each)
    cream cheese, softened
2 tablespoons bottled steak
    sauce

1/4 cup creamy salad dressing
1 clove garlic or 1 teaspoon
    garlic powder
1 small onion, finely chopped
2 cans (3-3/4 ounces each)
    smoked oysters, well-drained
    and chopped
3 cups chopped pecans, divided
3 tablespoons chili powder
Chopped fresh parsley

In mixer bowl, blend together cheese, steak sauce, salad dressing, garlic and onion. Stir in oysters and 1 cup of pecans. Shape into long cylinder (I use a French loaf baking pan). Roll in mixture of chili powder, remaining pecans and parsley. **Yield:** 1 18-inch log (2-1/2-in. diameter).

CHRISTMAS VEGETABLE SALAD
Mary Dean, Eau Claire, Wisconsin

(PICTURED ON PAGE 84)

DRESSING:
1-1/2 tablespoons fresh lemon juice
1-1/2 tablespoons white wine
    vinegar
4 tablespoons vegetable oil
1 teaspoon salt
1/2 teaspoon sugar
Freshly ground black pepper

2 cups thinly sliced cauliflower
1/2 cup sliced stuffed green olives
1/3 cup chopped green pepper
1/3 cup chopped red pepper

Put all dressing ingredients in jar; shake well. Combine cauliflower, olives and peppers in glass bowl; pour dressing over all. Marinate in refrigerator for several hours or overnight. **Yield:** 6-8 servings.

MOSTACCIOLI
Nancy Mundhenke, Kinsley, Kansas

(PICTURED ON PAGE 85)

1-1/2 pounds bulk Italian sausage
4 cups meatless spaghetti sauce
1 pound mostaccioli, cooked
    and drained
1 beaten egg
15 ounces ricotta cheese
8 ounces shredded Mozzarella
    cheese
1/2 cup freshly grated Romano
    cheese

In a Dutch oven, brown sausage; drain. Stir in spaghetti sauce and mostaccioli; set aside. In a bowl, combine egg, ri-

cotta and Mozzarella. In a 13-in. x 9-in. x 2-in. baking pan or 2-1/2- to 3-qt. casserole, spread one-half of the mostaccioli mixture; layer cheese mixture over all; top with remaining mostaccioli mixture. Bake, covered, at 375° for 40 minutes. Top with Romano cheese; bake 5 minutes more or until mixture is heated through. Garnish with fresh basil. **Yield:** 10-12 servings.

POLISH PIEROGI
Adeline Piscitelli, Sayreville, New Jersey

(PICTURED ON PAGE 85)

DOUGH:
4 cups all-purpose flour
2 eggs
1/2 cup sour cream
1 teaspoon salt
2/3 cup warm water
POTATO FILLING:
3 medium potatoes, cooked,
    drained and mashed, about
    1 pound
1/2 medium onion, chopped
1/4 cup butter
Salt and pepper to taste
CHEESE FILLING:
1 pound dry cottage cheese
2 eggs, beaten
1/2 teaspoon salt
1/4 cup melted butter
SAUCE:
1 large onion, chopped
1/2 cup butter

To make dough, mix flour, eggs, sour cream, salt and water (a little at a time). Knead dough until firm and elastic; cover with a bowl and let rest 10 minutes. For potato filling, prepare potatoes; set aside. For cheese filling, combine ingredients and mix. Divide dough into three parts. On floured surface, roll dough to 1/8-in. thick; cut into 3-in. rounds with cutter. Place a small spoonful of filling in center of each round; fold and press edges together firmly to seal. Drop pierogi in simmering chicken bouillon with 1 teaspoon oil. Do not crowd. Simmer for 15 minutes, stirring gently with wooden spoon to prevent sticking. Remove with slotted spoon; drain well. Saute onion and butter until golden. Placed drained pierogi in casserole and pour onion/butter mixture over all. Garnish with brown mushrooms. **Yield:** 7 dozen.

SWISS 'N' CRAB SUPPER PIE

Kathy Crow, Cordova, Alaska

(PICTURED ON PAGE 85)

1 unbaked 9-in. pie crust *or* pastry-lined 9-1/2-in. tart pan with removable bottom
1 can (7-1/2 ounces) crab, drained, flaked and cartilage removed
1 cup shredded Swiss cheese
2 green onions, sliced thin
3 beaten eggs
1 cup light cream *or* evaporated milk
1/2 teaspoon salt
1/2 teaspoon grated lemon peel
1/4 teaspoon dry mustard
Dash mace
1/4 cup sliced unblanched almonds

Line unpricked pastry shell with heavy foil; fill with dry beans. Bake pastry at 450° for 5 minutes; take from oven, remove beans and foil. Arrange crab evenly over partially baked crust. Top with cheese and green onions. Combine remaining ingredients *except almonds*; pour over base. Top with almonds. Bake at 325° for 45 minutes or until set. Remove from oven; let stand 10 minutes before serving. **Yield:** 10 servings.

SWEDISH MEATBALLS

Emily Gould, Hawarden, Iowa

(PICTURED ON PAGE 85)

2/3 cup evaporated milk
2/3 cup chopped onion
1/4 cup fine dry bread crumbs
1/2 teaspoon salt
1/2 teaspoon allspice
Dash pepper
1 pound ground round
2 teaspoons butter
2 beef bouillon cubes
1 cup boiling water
1/2 cup cold water
2 tablespoons all-purpose flour
1 cup evaporated milk
1 tablespoon lemon juice

Combine 2/3 cup evaporated milk, onion, crumbs, salt, allspice and pepper. Add meat; mix well, chill. Shape meat mixture into 1-in. balls. In large skillet, brown meatballs in butter. Dissolve bouillon cubes in boiling water; pour over meatballs and bring to boil over medium heat. Cover; simmer for 15 minutes. Meanwhile, blend together

cold water and flour. Remove meatballs from skillet, skim fat from pan juices and reserve juices. Stir 1 cup evaporated milk and flour/water mixture into pan juices in skillet; cook, uncovered, over low heat, stirring until sauce thickens. Return meatballs to skillet. Stir in lemon juice. Serve with cooked noodles that have been tossed with poppy seeds and butter. **Yield:** 3-1/2 dozen 1-inch meatballs.

ORANGE APPEAL

Billie Moss, El Sobrante, California

(PICTURED ON PAGE 86)

8 to 10 large oranges, any variety
4 tablespoons orange juice concentrate *or* orange flavored liqueur
1/2 cup coconut, shredded
1/2 cup blanched almonds, sliced
1/2 cup confectioners' sugar

Peel oranges, removing as much white membrane as possible. Cut in crosswise slices 1/4-inch thick *or* section as pictured. Arrange one-half of the orange slices or sections overlapping on large platter or in bottom of round glass bowl. Sprinkle with concentrate/liqueur, coconut, almonds and one-half of confectioners' sugar. Top with remaining oranges. Sprinkle with remaining sugar. Chill until serving time. Serve chilled on glass plates with tea cookies and coffee. **Yield:** 8 servings.

WHITE CHRISTMAS CANDY

Carol Hammond, Helena, Alabama

(PICTURED ON PAGE 86)

2 pounds white chocolate*
1/2 pound red and green peppermint stick crunch** *or* crushed candy canes *or* crushed peppermint candies

Melt chocolate over medium/low heat, stirring until smooth. Remove from heat; stir in crunch. Spread on parchment-paper-lined cookie sheets; chill in refrigerator 8-10 minutes. Break into small pieces; store in airtight containers. **Yield:** 2-1/2 pounds.

*White chocolate is available in candy and cake making specialty stores.

**Peppermint stick crunch is available in 1 pound packages through Country Kitchen, Fort Wayne, IN 46808. Call (219) 482-4835 to order by phone.

SHORTBREAD

Mrs. Allen Swenson, Camdenton, Missouri

(PICTURED ON PAGE 86)

1/2 pound sweet butter, softened (*do not* substitute margarine)
1/2 teaspoon salt
1/2 cup granulated sugar
1/2 cup sifted confectioners' sugar
2 cups flour
1/2 cup cornstarch

In mixing bowl, cream together butter, salt and both sugars. Gradually blend in flour and cornstarch which have been sifted together. Shape dough into a 15-in. x 2-in. x 1-in. rectangle; chill. Slice cookies 1/4-inch thick; place on ungreased cookie sheet. Make two fork prints on each cookie. Bake at 325° for 15-18 minutes. Don't overbake—*cookies will not brown.* Cool on wire rack. **Yield:** 5 dozen cookies.

WHIPPED CREAM KRUMKAKE

Imelda Nesteby, Decorah, Iowa

(PICTURED ON PAGE 86)

3 large eggs
1 cup sugar
1/2 cup sweet butter, *melted*
1/2 cup whipping cream, *whipped*
1/2 teaspoon nutmeg
1-1/2 cups all-purpose flour
Sweet butter for krumkake plates

Beat eggs in mixing bowl until very light. Add sugar gradually, beating to blend. Slowly add melted butter, then whipped cream and nutmeg. Mix in flour. (Dough will be consistency of cookie dough.) Chill dough thoroughly. Preheat krumkake plates over medium heat for about 10 minutes or until a drop of water "dances" when dropped on plates. Brush plates with sweet butter; place 1 slightly rounded tablespoon dough in center of lower plate; close iron and press handles together. If excess dough comes out sides, remove with table knife. Bake for about 30 seconds; flip iron and bake for about 30 seconds on other side. Remove krumkake and immediately roll over cone-shaped form. Place seam side down on parchment paper to cool; remove form. Fill cooled cones with sweetened whipped cream, if desired. Serve immediately. **Yield:** About 3 dozen krumkake.

STUFFED DATES
Dorothy Pepper, Thermal, California

(PICTURED ON PAGE 88)

12 large dates, suitable for stuffing
1 package (3 ounces) cream cheese, softened
3 tablespoons orange marmalade
Walnut halves

Carefully cut dates in half; remove pits. Set aside. Combine cream cheese and marmalade until smooth. Toast walnut halves in 350° oven for about 10 minutes; cool. Fill date halves with cream cheese mixture using small spoon. Top each with a walnut half. Store, covered, in refrigerator. **Yield:** 12 stuffed dates.

ORANGE SUGARED PECANS
Murri Mills, Brady, Texas

(PICTURED ON PAGE 88)

1 cup brown sugar (firmly packed)
3 tablespoons evaporated milk
1 tablespoon butter
1 teaspoon freshly grated orange peel
2 cups pecan halves

In small heavy saucepan, combine the sugar and evaporated milk. Cook over medium heat to 234° (soft-ball stage), stirring occasionally. Add butter and orange peel; stir to blend. Add pecan halves; stir until all are coated. Spread the pecans on parchment paper or a greased cookie sheet. When the candy coating is firm, gently break pecans apart. Store in covered containers. **Yield:** 4 cups.

CHOCOLATE ALMOND TRUFFLES
Arla Railsback, New Richmond, Wisconsin

(PICTURED ON PAGE 88)

1/2 cup heavy whipping cream
3-1/2 tablespoons sweet butter
8 ounces semisweet chocolate chips
1/4 teaspoon almond flavoring *or* 1/4 cup Amaretto liqueur
Finely ground toasted almonds, chocolate sprinkles, chopped shredded coconut, cocoa powder

or confectioners' sugar for coating

In medium saucepan, heat cream and butter over medium-high heat, stirring until butter melts and mixture comes just to a boil. Remove pan from heat; add chocolate and stir until completely melted. Stir in flavoring/liqueur. Cover, placing paper towels between lid and saucepan to absorb moisture, if desired. Chill at least 3 hours, stirring three to four times as mixture cools and thickens. Remove about 1-1/2 teaspoons at a time and roll into balls. Roll balls in choice of coating. Refrigerate until ready to serve. Store in refrigerator. **Yield:** About 3-1/2 dozen balls, 1 in. each.

HIGH ALTITUDE HINT: Live at a high altitude? Remember that for every 500 ft. above sea level, candy syrups should be cooked to 1° *lower* than temperature indicated in recipes. For example, if a recipe specifies 234° and you live at 2,000 ft., cook syrup only to 230°.

ORANGE/CHOCOLATE SUGARPLUMS
Evelyn Skaggs, Nixa, Missouri

(PICTURED ON PAGE 89)

2 cups coarsely chopped pecans
2 cups coarsely chopped unblanched almonds
1 cup orange marmalade
1/2 cup flaked coconut
1 package (8 ounces) semisweet chocolate
1 egg, beaten
Confectioners' sugar

In a large bowl, mix pecans, almonds, marmalade and coconut. Set aside. In small saucepan, melt chocolate at low temperature; remove from heat and cool 15 minutes. Beat egg into chocolate until mixture is smooth. Stir chocolate into nut mixture; chill 1 hour or until firm enough to handle. Shape into walnut-size balls. Roll in confectioners' sugar. Store, covered, in refrigerator. **Yield:** About 5 dozen balls.

SPICED MIXED NUTS
Joanne Warner, Baldwin, Wisconsin

(PICTURED ON PAGE 89)

1 egg white, lightly beaten
1 teaspoon water
1 jar (8 ounces) dry roasted peanuts

1/2 cup unblanched whole almonds
1/2 cup walnut *or* pecan halves
3/4 cup sugar
1 tablespoon pumpkin pie spice

In large bowl, combine egg white and water. Add nuts; toss to coat. Combine sugar and spice; sprinkle over the nuts and toss until well coated. Place nuts in single layer on lightly greased baking sheet. Bake at 300° for 20-25 minutes. Immediately transfer the nuts to waxed paper; cool. Break up large clusters. Store in a covered container. **Yield:** 6 cups.

TWO-TONE FUDGE
Lavonne Sullivan, Topeka, Kansas

(PICTURED ON PAGE 89)

2 cups brown sugar, firmly packed
1 cup granulated sugar
1 cup evaporated milk
1/2 cup sweet butter
1 jar (7 ounces) marshmallow creme
1 teaspoon vanilla
1 package (6 ounces) butterscotch chips
1 cup coarsely chopped walnuts, *divided*
1 package (6 ounces) semisweet chocolate chips

In saucepan, combine the brown sugar, granulated sugar, evaporated milk and butter. Bring to full boil over moderate heat, stirring constantly. Boil for 10 minutes, stirring occasionally. Remove from heat. Add marshmallow creme and vanilla; stir until mixture is smooth. Remove *2 cups* of hot mixture; add butterscotch chips and *1/2 cup* walnuts. Stir until chips are melted and mixture is smooth. Pour evenly into greased 9-in.-square pan; place in freezer to chill while preparing second layer. To *remaining* hot mixture, add chocolate chips and *1/2 cup* walnuts. Stir until chips are melted and mixture is smooth. Pour evenly over the butterscotch mixture in pan. Chill until firm. **Yield:** 2-1/2 lbs. candy.

HANDY CANDY HINTS:
- Insert the candy thermometer when mixture boils, not before.
- Don't double candy recipes, as this changes the cooking time.
- Stir and beat with a wooden spoon for safety and comfort.

MICROWAVE LECHE QUEMADA
Mildred Kneupper, New Braunfels, Texas

(PICTURED ON PAGE 89)

2 cups pecans (small or broken pieces)
1/2 cup sweet butter
2/3 cup brown sugar, firmly packed
1 can (14 ounces) sweetened condensed milk
1 teaspoon vanilla

Place pecans on large glass plate and microwave (MW) on HIGH (100% power) for 8 minutes, stirring at 2-minute intervals. Set aside. In 8-cup measure, MW butter on HIGH for 1 minute. Stir in brown sugar and milk until blended. MW on HIGH for 7 minutes, stirring at 2-minute intervals. Beat with wooden spoon until stiff, about 5 minutes. Stir in vanilla and roasted pecans. Spread in lightly buttered 8-in.-square glass dish; chill until firm. Cut into squares. **Yield:** 1-1/2 lbs.

CANDIED CITRUS PEELS
Mary Malinowski, Lee Center, New York

(PICTURED ON PAGE 89)

2 cups fresh orange, grapefruit or lemon peels (about 4 oranges)
Cold water
SYRUP:
1/2 cup water
1 cup sugar
Confectioners' sugar
CHOCOLATE COATING:
8 ounces semisweet chocolate chips
4 ounces unsweetened chocolate
2-inch x 1-inch x 1/2-inch piece of paraffin wax

Using a metal zester or similar tool, cut peels from fruits in 1/4-in.-wide strips 3 in. long. Place peels in heavy saucepan; cover with cold water. Bring slowly to boiling; reduce heat and simmer 10 minutes. Drain; repeat boiling process three-five times, draining well each time. (This cooks the peels and eliminates bitterness of membrane.) In separate saucepan, combine sugar and water; cook till clear. Add peels; boil gently until all syrup is absorbed and peels are transparent. Roll peels in confectioners' sugar; place on cooling rack to dry. Combine chocolate coating ingredients in top of

double boiler; melt together over simmering water until smooth. Dip half of each peel in chocolate; cool on rack sprayed with vegetable spray. Store, covered, in refrigerator. **Yield:** About 3 cups.

EASY MICROWAVE CARAMELS
Darleen Worm, Fond Du Lac, Wisconsin

(PICTURED ON PAGE 90)

1 cup sweet butter
2-1/3 cups (1 pound) brown sugar, firmly packed
1 cup light corn syrup
1 can (14 ounces) sweetened condensed milk
1/8 teaspoon salt
1 teaspoon vanilla
1/2 cup chopped walnuts, optional

In 2-qt. microwave-safe pitcher, combine butter, sugar, syrup, milk and salt. Microwave (MW) on HIGH (100% power) 3 to 4 minutes, stirring once after about 2 minutes. When butter is melted, stir well. Attach *microwave* candy thermometer. MW on HIGH about 14 minutes or until mixture reaches 245° (firm-ball stage). No stirring is needed. Remove from microwave; stir in vanilla and walnuts. Allow to stand for 10 minutes, stirring well several times. Pour into buttered 13-in. x 9-in. x 2-in. pan (smaller 11-in. x 7-in. x 1-1/2-in. pan yields thicker candy as shown in photo). Refrigerate until cool. Invert pan. Carefully tap out whole block of candy; cut in squares. Wrap in wax paper and store in refrigerator. (Can also freeze.) **Yield:** About 2-3/4 lbs.

AUNT ROSE'S FANTASTIC BUTTER TOFFEE
Rosie Kimberlin, Los Angeles, California

(PICTURED ON PAGE 90)

2 cups whole unblanched almonds (about 10 ounces), *divided*
11 ounces milk chocolate, *divided*
2 sticks sweet butter
1 cup sugar
3 tablespoons cold water

Spread almonds in a pan and toast in 350° oven for about 10 minutes, shaking pan occasionally. Cool nuts. Grind milk chocolate fine in food processor—*do not overprocess*. Set aside. Chop

nuts coarse in food processor. Sprinkle *1 cup* nuts over bottom of greased 15-in. x 10-in. x 1-in. jelly roll pan. Sprinkle *1 cup* ground chocolate over nuts. Set aside. In heavy saucepan, combine butter, sugar and water; cook over medium heat, stirring occasionally, until the mixture reaches 290° (soft-crack stage). *Very quickly* pour mixture over nuts and chocolate. Sprinkle remaining chocolate over toffee; top with remaining nuts. Chill and break into pieces. **Yield:** About 2 lbs.

MOUNDS BALLS
Kathy Dorman, Snover, Michigan

(PICTURED ON PAGE 90)

1/2 pound sweet butter
1 pound confectioners' sugar
1 pound flaked coconut
1/2 can (7 ounces) sweetened condensed milk *or* 1/2 cup
1 cup chopped walnuts
1 teaspoon vanilla
CHOCOLATE COATING:
1 package (12 ounces) semisweet chocolate chips
4 ounces unsweetened chocolate squares
2-inch x 1-inch x 1/2-inch piece paraffin wax
Round wood toothpicks
Styrofoam sheets

In mixing bowl, cream together butter and sugar. Add coconut, milk, walnuts and vanilla; stir until blended. Chill until slightly firm; roll into walnut-sized balls. Insert a toothpick in each ball. Place balls on cookie sheets; freeze. In double boiler over simmering water, melt chocolate chips, chocolate squares and paraffin wax. Keep warm over hot water. Using picks as handles, dip frozen balls into chocolate mixture; stick picks upright into wax paper-covered Styrofoam sheet. Chill until firm. Remove picks and package candy in individual paper liners. (May also be frozen.) **Yield:** About 7 dozen candies.

DRYING RACK: Making chocolate-dipped candies? First prepare 2 or 3 small wooden boards by drilling rows of tiny holes (large enough for round toothpicks). Then insert a toothpick in each candy, dip, stick the toothpick in board and chill until chocolate sets. As an alternative, use Styrofoam squares to hold toothpicked candies after dipping.

QUICK TURTLES
Fern Lockwood, Daytona Beach, Florida

1-1/2 cups pecan halves
1 package (14 ounces) vanilla caramels
5 bars milk chocolate (1-1/2 ounces each), broken into squares

Arrange pecans in clusters of 3 or 4 halves 2 in. apart on a greased baking sheet. Top each cluster with one caramel, slightly flattened. Bake at 300° for 7 minutes or until caramels soften. Remove to waxed paper. Flatten caramels with spatula; top each candy with 1 milk chocolate bar while still warm. Spread chocolate when melted. Refrigerate a few minutes until chocolate hardens. **Yield:** 4 dozen turtles.

DATE NUT BALLS
Myrtle McSwan, Indio, California

1 cup pitted dates
1 cup raisins
1/2 cup dried apricots
1/2 cup pitted prunes or figs
Unsweetened orange juice to moisten
Flaked coconut or chopped walnuts

In food grinder, grind together dates, raisins, apricots, prunes/figs. Combine with orange juice in 2-qt. mixing bowl. Roll into bite-size balls. Roll in coconut or in nuts. Refrigerate, covered, until time to serve. **Yield:** About 2 dozen.

MICROWAVE PEANUT BRITTLE
Sue Moore, Hartwell, Georgia

1 cup raw peanuts
1 cup sugar
1/2 cup white corn syrup
1/8 teaspoon salt
1 teaspoon butter
1 teaspoon vanilla
1 teaspoon baking soda

In a 1-1/2-qt. casserole, stir together peanuts, sugar, syrup and salt. Microwave (MW) on HIGH (100% power) for 4 minutes; stir well and MW for 4 minutes more. Stir in the butter and vanilla. MW

2 minutes longer. Add baking soda and quickly stir until light and foamy. *Immediately* pour onto lightly greased cookie sheet, spreading out thin. Cool; break into small pieces. Store in an airtight container. **Yield:** About 1 lb.

BLUEBERRY CLUSTERS
June Pothier, Norristown, Pennsylvania

2 cups (11-1/2 ounces) milk chocolate chips
1/4 cup butter or margarine
2 cups fresh blueberries, washed and dried
1-1/2-inch paper candy liners

Over hot (not boiling) water, combine the chocolate and butter. Stir until melted and mixture is smooth. Remove from heat. Place 1 teaspoon of melted chocolate in paper candy liner. Add 6 to 8 blueberries; top with 2 teaspoons chocolate, making sure the blueberries are well coated. Chill for 20 to 30 minutes. Serve at room temperature up to 1 hour; store in refrigerator. **Yield:** About 2-1/2 dozen candies.

MACADAMIA NUT FUDGE
Vicki Fioranelli, Cleveland, Mississippi

(PICTURED ON PAGE 90)

3 cups crushed macadamia nuts, divided, or toasted pecans
4-1/2 cups granulated sugar
1/2 cup sweet butter
1 can (12 or 13 ounces) evaporated milk
1 box (12 ounces) German sweet chocolate squares, chopped
1 package (12 ounces) semisweet chocolate chips
1 jar (7 ounces) marshmallow creme
1 teaspoon salt (omit if using salted nuts)
2 teaspoons vanilla

Crush macadamia nuts by placing in a plastic bag and pounding with mallet. Set aside. Grease two 9-in.-square pans or line with waxed paper. Combine sugar, butter and milk in heavy pan; bring to a gentle boil. Cook for 5 minutes, stirring constantly. Remove from heat; add remaining ingredients *except* 1 cup nuts. Pour fudge into prepared pans; sprinkle remaining nuts over top and press in lightly. Chill until firm; cut in squares. **Yield:** About 5 lbs.

GIFT-GIVING: Empty Christmas card boxes make nice personal-size candy containers. For make-ahead gifts, cover the boxes in foil, fill with chunks of candy like Rocky Road, then stack boxes in a heavy plastic bag and freeze. Later, thaw and add a red bow and a sprig of holly.

● Shop rummage sales throughout the year for pretty dishes and cute tins or trays for candy-giving. At holidays or special occasions, fill with home-made goodies, cover with plastic wrap and say, "Keep the dish!"

EASY SPICED NUTS
Coral Rhoda, Holland, Michigan

1 egg white
1 teaspoon cold water
1 pound (4 cups) pecan halves
1/2 cup sugar
1/4 teaspoon salt
1/2 teaspoon cinnamon

Beat the egg white slightly; add the water. Beat until frothy but not stiff. Pour over pecans in a large bowl; stir until nuts are coated. Mix sugar, salt and cinnamon. Sprinkle over pecans; mix well. Pour into a 13-in. x 9-in. x 2-in. buttered pan; bake at 250° 1 hour. Stir once or twice while baking. **Yield:** About 6 cups.

WHITE CHOCOLATE PRETZELS
Jenny Riegsecker, Delta, Ohio

12 ounces white chocolate, chopped
6 ounces semisweet chocolate chips
2 to 3 dozen twisted pretzels, all whole
Finely chopped nuts, if desired

Melt white chocolate in microwave or double boiler. With tongs, dip pretzels, one at a time, in chocolate. Let excess chocolate run off back into pan. Place dipped pretzels on waxed paper to cool; chill to harden slightly. Melt the semisweet chocolate; cool several minutes. Using a pastry bag with small round pastry tip (or a plastic bag with the tip snipped off or a large spoon), drizzle dark chocolate squiggles over coated pretzels. Immediately sprinkle with nuts, if desired. Chill. **Yield:** 2-3 dozen.

INDEX

A

B

C